AF560814

Evaluating Science Textbooks at Secondary Level

Evaluating Science Textbooks at Secondary Level

A Study in Odisha

Rashmirekha Das

₹995; US$ 33
ISBN: 978-93-91978-92-1

2024
First Published in India

Evaluating Science Textbooks at Secondary Level: A Study in Odisha

Published by:
SHIPRA PUBLICATIONS
LG 18-19, Pankaj Central Market
I.P. Ext., Patparganj, Delhi 110092, India
011 47322068, 2223 5152/6152; 96500 28065
info@shiprapublication.com
www.shiprapublication.com

Acknowledgments

I am deeply indebted to Almighty Lord Jagannath who has been a constant source of my inner and outer strength.

I express my thanks to Dr. Nirupama Barpanda, former principal and the faculty members of Dr PMIASE, Sambalpur for their support throughout the study.

After the blessings of Almighty, I express my gratitude to three jewels of my life, my better half Mr. Annada Prasad Rayguru and two of my sons Rishiraj Yatharth, Yashraj Shreyansh. They always give me courage and never complain for any negligence towards them, rather they try their best to adjust with the given circumstances. I am also grateful to my parents Late Gadadhar Rayguru, Sanjukta Rayguru, Late Dhruba Charan Das, Swarna Lata Nayak, my uncle Gangadhar Nayak and his daughters—Gugul, Ripal, Simpal for their constant care, persistent encouragement, personal involvement and moral support throughout this study. A special thanks goes to a few of my well-wishers Baby didi, Apa, Mitu, younger brother Barada Prasanna, Padma Kar, Girija Bhusan Mishra and Pravati didi. The researcher also thanks all her friends Kuni, Eltix, Anu, Sushree, Kajol, Sarmistha and Anita who always encouraged me for completion of my Ph.D. work.

Last but not the least I am thankful to Prof. Lokanath Mishra who has been showing me path to overcome the hurricane task to settle in a very simple and easier way. He has not only supervised my thesis work but also encouraged me to conclude the work within the schedule time frame.

Dr. Rashmirekha Das

Contents

Abbreviations

BSE	Board of Secondary Education
DIKSHA	Digital Infrastructure for Knowledge Sharing
HOT	Higher Order Thinking
NCERT	National Council of Educational Research and Training
NCF	National Curriculum Framework
NEP	National Education Policy
OAV	Odisha Adarsha Vidyalaya
OSBTP	Odisha State Bureau of Textbook Preparation
OSEPA	Odisha School Education Programme Authority
QR Code	Quick Response Code
SCERT	State Council of Educational Research and Training
SCF	State Curriculum Framework
TBPM	Textbook Production and Marketing

I

Science Education and Textbooks at Secondary Level – An Introduction

National Education Policy and Curriculum Framework

Introduction

Education is a process which enables a person to acquire knowledge of the world around us. It gives individuals the information, capacities, ability, and data they need to figure out their commitments to their families, networks and country. Education helps in developing their capabilities to fight against injustice, violence, corruption and other wrong practices of the society. Education prepares people to develop new ideas which enable creativity to adapt to the new situations in a better way. Modern world is a new industrial world. People need quality education to survive in this industrialized competitive world.

Education helps in removing poverty. If a person is educated, he can be better prepared in getting good job and can fulfil basic needs of his family. An educated person can distinguish between good and bad, and will never involve in domestic violence and maintain healthy human relationships. He can lead a safe and secure life and work towards self-reliance. It helps a person to be aware of political field and can lead a secure citizen life.

Proper education helps a person in developing communication with other people. He can deliver speech in a public gathering, can present research papers in seminars, symposiums and can discuss issues properly. Realizing the importance of education, formal schooling has been set up in our society. As per the constitutional obligations all the children are expected to complete formal schooling within a fixed time frame and with specified objectives.

The schooling process is directly concerned with the development of the child. The schools are expected to provide academic opportunities through which the child will acquire desirable qualities and it will be helpful in developing his personality in a society as per accepted norms and behaviour. Teachers who are more knowledgeable, trained, and interact with children shape personality of the children well. The formal education in schools has been designed to bring social transformation and is an important means of national development. According to Gandhiji, Education is more comprehensive than its literal meaning. Education is significant for a youngster's entire development. Education specialists and logicians have reached the resolution that educational plan, course readings, and instructors are critical to a kid's general turn of events, including their physical, mental, social, moral, profound and social prosperity. As per the report of Education Commission (1964-66) in our education system at school level, it is essential to include science as one of the courses in the curriculum.

> *There is of course one thing about which we feel no doubt or hesitation: education, science based and in coherence with Indian Culture and Values, can alone provide the foundation as also the instrument for the nation's progress, security and welfare.*

However, in recent decades, it has been seen that there is a retreat of public reasoning in the public sphere that has helped in the culmination of and rise of anti-science attitude and religious revivalism in public life (Raina, 2016).

School Education as per National Education Policy 2020

This policy envisages that the 10+2 structure in school education will be modified with a new pedagogical and curricular restructuring of 5+3+3+4 covering ages 3-18 as shown in the representative. Currently, children in the age group of 3-6 are not covered in the 10+2 structure as Class I begins at age 6. In the new 5+3+3+4 structure, a strong base of Early Childhood Care and Education (ECCE) from age 3 is also included, which is aimed at promoting better overall learning, development, and well-being.The 5+3+3+4 education approach demonstrates how to structure an entire schooling course to enhance accessibility, admission, responsibility, and universalization at the preschool level while also delivering top-quality education as it also extends the approach of the Right to Education Act to incorporate those aged between 3 to 18. To align with the existing urban education plan, children enroll in playschools, then move on to schools where they complete two years of kindergarten classes and go to school for 12 years.

Aims and Objectives of the National Education Policy 2020

Main aims and objectives of the NEP 2020 are as follows:

1. To promote multilingualism.
2. To enhance the quality of education and research in India.
3. To make India a global education hub.
4. To provide equitable quality education to all students irrespective of their social, cultural, and economic backgrounds.
5. To make the curriculum flexible and within the reach of children.
6. To make overall development of children i.e., physical, social, emotional and cognitive development.
7. To foster critical thinking and ethical values among learners.
8. To prepare the children for the future.

NEP 2020 focuses on cognitive development, character building, creating holistic and all-round development. Itfocuses towards learning how to learn. Give less emphasis on rote learning. Students are given increased flexibility and choice of subjects to study. There is no hard separation among curricular, extracurricular and co-curricular among arts, science and humanities or in between vocational or academic stream.

Teachers truly shape the future of our children, therefore, the future of our nation. It is because of this noblest role that the teacher in India was the most respected member of society. Only the very best and most learned became teachers. Society gave teachers, or gurus, what they needed in order to pass on their knowledge, skills, and ethics optimally to students. Today, however, the status of the teacher has undoubtedly and unfortunately dropped. The quality of training, recruitment, deployment, service conditions and empowerment of teachers is not where it should be, and consequently, the quality and motivation of teachers does not reach the standards where it could be. The high respect for teachers and the high status of the teaching profession must be revived and restored for the very best to be inspired to enter the profession, for teachers to be well-motivated and empowered to innovate, and for education to therefore reach the heights and levels that are truly required to ensure the best possible future for our children and our nation.

Importance of Science Education in School Curriculum

Curriculum plays a significant role in achieving the specified objectives of any formal education system. The word curriculum has been derived from Latin word 'curricula' which means to run. In a formal schooling, it is a race adopted by school for reaching certain goals. It enriches the learning experiences of the learner. For this a series of manifold activities are designed by the school inside the classroom and outside the classroom including in the laboratory, in the playground, in all formal and informal activities of the school. Learning is the outcome of all experiences gathered by the learner in the school. Thus, curriculum is the total of experiences the students undergo under the direction of schools. It includes not only the content of the books but all the designed activities of the authority of the schools. Curriculum is a process and not a finished product. It empowers the teachers what to teach and how to teach. It is closely related to the age and maturity level of pupils where various ideas are introduced.

On the basis of guidelines suggested in the curriculum of a particular class syllabus is prepared. It is meant to act as a tool for teachers and students to follow guidance about the subject to be taught for a particular class. Each syllabus has been prepared by experts in a particular subject. Science education is a key requirement of education for all learners irrespective of time. Although only a small percentage of students are destined to follow scientific careers, every person needs some understanding of mathematics, science and technology to succeed in today's technologically oriented world (Leitte, 2002; Singer & Tuomi, 2003; Department of Education of South Africa, 2003a; Jenkins, 2004; Lisichkin, 2007; Lederman, 2008). Consequently, excellent science training is pivotal to guaranteeing that students are ready for callings in science as well as that the country has a general population that is experimentally educated and able to do "addressing the worldwide difficulties that mankind by and by faces" (Wieman, 2007). In this regard science education aids in the realization of the learner's potential and contributes to the development of our country's human resources (Department of Education of South Africa, 2001; Reddy, 2006).

Before independence science teaching was not so important in school curriculum. But now-a-days science teaching has acquired a suitable, respectful and proud place in school curriculum. This is a compulsory subject in most of the secondary schools' curriculum. During schooling, students are curious by nature. They want to explore new things. It is an active subject with practical activities. The principles and ideas of science are of great importance to students in three ways. First, in their personal lives: by studying science and scientific principles they can adopt healthy lifestyle. Second, by adopting a scientific attitude they can lead a better civic life.

They can actively participate in social decisions. Third, in their economic life they can have better opportunity in various job opportunities by reading science-related subjects.

Science develops the power of reasoning, thinking, curiosity, open-mindedness and develops a scientific attitude. Thus, it could be aimed as an instrument for social change towards a better society. Yashpal (1992) is of the opinion that, instead of considering science as an extraneous activity and as a tool for providing the means to a good life which is borrowed from outside, it should be treated as a part of the culture of society. It should be integrated into our living and thinking. It should be connected to our spirit of questioning, so that problems related to our day-to-day living can be solved.

The knowledge and skills required by a modern householder in dealing with electrical, plumbing a person needs the required skills for this teaching science is a must. For science teaching in schools, textbook is necessary. Textbook can play an important role in addressing the problem of inadequately qualified teachers (Huberand, 2001; Reddy, 2005; Newton & Newton, 2006). Research shows that textbooks are among the most cost-effective ways of improving classroom practice (Verspoor, 1991; Asmal, 2002; Lubben, Campbell, Kasanda, Kapenda, Gaoseb & Kanjeo-Marenga, 2003). Textbooks are the source for providing the necessary prescribed content material to the student of a particular class (Garte & Despande, 1997). The textbooks provide opportunity to realize the aims and objectives of science instructions and the aims and objectives of the course in general (Baker & Piburn, 1991). The textbook of science has to achieve the overall descent requirement of society. Furthermore, research has shown that using well designed textbooks or curriculum material can positively influence teaching beliefs and practices, aiding curriculum implementation (Davis, 2009; Newton and Newton, 2006; Davis, 2003a; Izsak and Sherin, 2003; McKenney, 2001).

Aims and Objectives of Teaching Science at Secondary Level

All subjects during secondary stage are taught with some specific aims. Aims specify ways to reach the goal. In our country attempts have been made from time to time to think about the aims of teaching science at different stages in school education. One such attempt was made in 1956 at Tara Devi Hills through an All-India seminar organized on the science topic for teaching in secondary schools. The other attempts were made by Kothari commission in 1966. On the basis of their recommendations, it was derived that science imparts instructions for developing scientific attitude among the learners. It contributes in all round development of the child so that he/she should be encouraged as a socially useful and efficient citizen of the modern world. The school helps the pupils to acquire scientific knowledge to develop critical thinking, accurate observation, scientific method and scientific attitude amongst the pupils. Thus, school will prepare future scientific citizens in the modern world.

Aims

Based on the recommendations of all commissions the following aims can be set at the secondary stage (from class VIII to X).

1. To provide the students with a more profound comprehension of the science realities and standards (than in past illustrations).
2. To work on their ability for skillfully completing logical tests and to help them in acquiring further comprehension of how science is utilized.
3. To finish the requirements for further developed particular courses in technical studies and advances.
4. To offer understudies the right chance to foster their imaginative and unique reasoning abilities.
5. To give the students all the crucial logical skill and capacities that are helpful in everyday living.
6. To help them in securing and concentrating on a few common-sense logical leisure activities and relaxation exercises for useful pursuits.
7. To impart in them the legitimate outlook and conviction on the significance and meaning of science.

Objectives implies ways and means of achieving aims, should be gained in a definite and practical way. The teaching of science may be classified into exceptional objectives for supplementing definite learning experiences and has a noble effect in behavioural changes. These changes are expected from all the three behavioural domains. The three domains are: a) cognitive (knowing), b) conative (doing), and c) affective (feeling). The outcome of teaching science can be observed in all these three domains. The instructional objectives set for this purpose must be stated in behavioural terms.

Objectives

The major objectives of teaching science both physical and life sciences can be specified in behavioural terms in the following manner.

1. *Knowledge*: pupil acquires knowledge of the terms, facts, concepts, definitions, principles and processes related to physical and life sciences.
2. *Understanding*: pupils develop understanding of terms, facts, concepts, definitions, principles and processes related to physical and life sciences.
3. *Application*: pupil applies his knowledge and understanding of the subject physical and life sciences to the day-to-day life activities and to the new or unfamiliar situations.
4. *Skill*: The pupil develops mathematical skills, manipulative skills, drawing skills, dissecting skills, collecting, mounting and processing skills and many more.
5. *Interest*: The pupil develops interest in the world of physical and life sciences.
6. *Appreciation*: The pupil appreciates the contribution of sciences to human welfare which include food productivity, establishing improved health and hygiene, make life systematic, maintaining ecological balance and formulating procedures for controlling pollution of environment. Knowledge of life sciences develops the habit of sanitation, balanced diet and prevention of diseases. This also develops in individuals the ways and means of solving food problems, overpopulation, conservation, plant breeding, forestry, dairy science and food preservation.

Thus, it has been made a compulsory subject at secondary classes in most of the states of India including Odisha. The study of biological science is very important in every walk of human life. The students from secondary level should study this subject for a better future life.

National Curriculum Framework 2005 and Science Education

According to National Curriculum Framework 2005 (NCF 2005) science is a dynamic, growing collection of information, covering

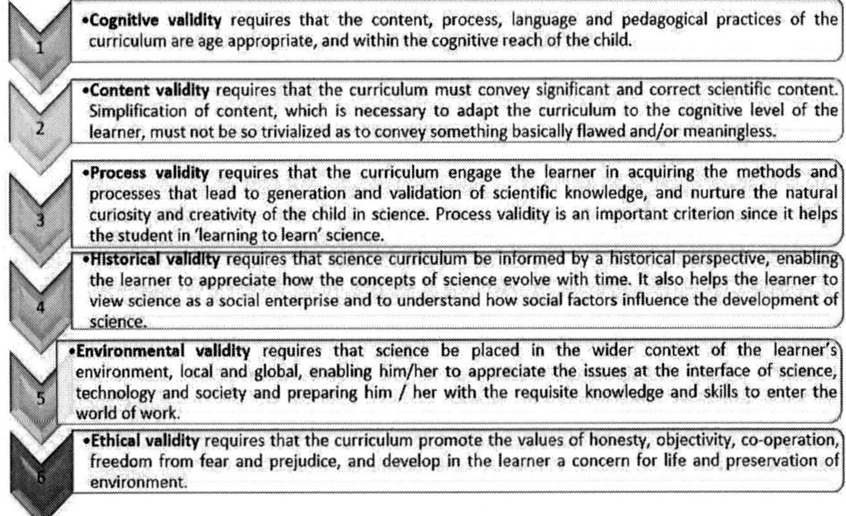

Figure 1.1 *Science Curriculum Validity Criteria Proposed by NCF 2005*

ever-new spaces of involvement. In a dynamic forward-looking society, science can play a really freeing job, assisting individuals with getting away from the endless loop of neediness, obliviousness and strange notion. The advances in science and innovation have changed conventional fields of work like farming and industry and prompted the rise of entirely new fields of work. Individuals today are confronted with an undeniably quick influencing world where the main abilities are adaptability, advancement and innovativeness. These various objectives must be remembered in forming science schooling. Science schooling is consistent with the kid, consistent with life and consistent with science.

NCF 2005 talks about the educational program of science at the optional stage, understudies ought to be taken part in learning science as a composite discipline, in working with hands and devices to configuration further developed mechanical modules than at the upper essential stage and in exercises and examinations on issues concerning the climate and wellbeing, including regenerative and sexual wellbeing. Precise trial and error as an instrument to find, confirm hypothetical standards, and dealing with locally huge tasks including science and innovation, are to be significant pieces of the educational plan at this stage. The investigates (Ninnes, 2000; Koppal and Caldwell, 2004; Merciful,

2008; McKinney, 2013) affirm the significance of science course readings and its examination.

NCF 2005 speaks about the six legitimacy models — mental, content, process, verifiable, natural, and moral — straightforwardly connect with the objectives of science schooling. To summarize, science training ought to empower the student to:

- know current realities and standards of science and its applications, reliable with the phase of mental turn of events;
- get what it takes and grasp the strategies and cycles that lead to the age and approval of logical information; and apply information on science to tackle issues;
- to help her consider science to be a social undertaking and to procure a verifiable and formative viewpoint of science;
- grasp issues at the convergence of science, innovation, and society and connect with the climate (the regular habitat, ancient rarities, and individuals), both locally and universally;
- collect the important innovative expertise and useful capacities prior to entering the labor force;
- support individuals' innate imagination, tasteful sense, and interest in science and innovation;
- incorporate the temperance's of honesty, trustworthiness, participation, worry forever, and natural security; and
- create a "logical attitude," or the limit with respect to objectivity, decisive idea, and the shortfall of dread and bias.

NCF 2005 additionally considered the meaning of science instruction and suggested legitimacy measures for approval of any science textbook. Each country sees science schooling as a valuable device for cultivating in understudies a logical outlook that will empower them to construct a libertarian world. It seems impossible without any science textbook that can encourage the advancement of solid logical information. Thus, dissecting the science textbook is essential. The specialist chose to lead a review to decide "what is the major cantered areas of science reading material examination in the 21st century and furthermore to investigate whether the science books have been written in a manner that satisfies the reason for science training." The researcher studied the literatures on the writing of science textbook.

As per NCF 2005, the development of creativity and imagination is the improvement of a feeling of request and imagination in researcher is one of the fundamental objectives of science training. To empower interest, curiosity, and imagination, NCF-2005 prompts the accompanying: Draw in understudies in learning exercises, logical fairs, tests, and undertaking work, as well as students' science congresses and extracurricular exercises. Put together science and innovation fairs at the nearby, locale, state, and public levels with the assistance of not-for-profit associations, instructor affiliations, and public and state level specialists. Make innovative and trial course materials, including course books, and inside assessment techniques.

As indicated by NCF 2005, reading material are the essential vehicle for conveying educational plan, consequently the accompanying variables should be considered: Empower the learners and teachers to broadly utilize textbook. Moreover, it pushes for the extension of science instruction. The stakeholders of secondary schools take part in the production of textbooks in general and biological science textbook in particular.

National Curriculum Framework 2023 and Science Education

Science is a dynamic body of knowledge that enables an understanding of the world around us through a process of inquiry. This process leads to acquisition of valid knowledge about the world, and of scientific values and capacities, such as formulating questions and hypotheses, inquiry, evidence-based thinking, creativity, understanding cause and effect relationships, and decision making.

In the school curriculum, children start learning the processes of science from the Foundational Stage itself. In the Preparatory Stage, they continue learning the processes of science, and observe simple patterns and relationships in their natural environment. This lays the basis for concepts related to science. Science is introduced as a separate curricular area only in the Middle Stage. In this Stage, the approach integrates Biology, Chemistry and Physics. This integrated approach develops fundamental capacities related to all disciplines, while using connections across disciplinary areas to help students make sense of their observations and experiences.

The integrated approach continues in the first two years of the Secondary Stage (Grades 9 and 10). In the next two years (Grades 11 and 12), a disciplinary approach is taken, with Physics, Chemistry and Biology being offered separately. Students get the opportunity to understand the nature of each discipline more deeply and develop specific competencies related to each. They also get the opportunity to explore their interest in taking the discipline up for further study. At all Stages, along with conceptual understanding, the process capacities of science are developed with increasing complexity, as the methods are learnt. Students would understand the world around them with increasing depth and would also be able to explore scientific questions at different levels, across the stages. They are able to strengthen the understanding acquired at earlier stages, and also learn to communicate this understanding in different ways. Connections with other curricular areas are also emphasised.

Science develops a valid understanding of the physical world, and develops other important capacities, along with values and dispositions. This in turn enables the meaningful participation of individuals in society and the world of work with scientific temper, critical and evidence-based thinking, asking fundamental questions, analysing practices and norms, and acting for necessary changes.

The world itself is undergoing rapid changes, and human beings need to adapt to these changes effectively, while also being the creators of change. It is this dynamic in which science contributes to societal, human, technological, and economic development through new knowledge and innovation. With this context, the aims of science education are:

a. *Developing understanding of scientific knowledge*: Students develop an understanding of the concepts, principles, laws, and theories, and process capacities of science in keeping with their developmental stage. They use this understanding to explore and make sense of the world independently and in collaboration with peers.
b. *Developing the ability to use the scientific method*: Students develop the ability to put forth arguments, predict, analyse, draw logical conclusions, take decisions and evaluate situations using the scientific method.
c. *Developing an understanding of how scientific knowledge evolves*: Students develop a historical and developmental perspective of science. They understand that scientific knowledge developed as a result of the efforts of many individuals across many years. They also understand how the methods of science evolved over time.

d. *Developing an understanding of the connection between science and other curricular areas*: Students view science as part of a larger canvas of disciplines. They become aware of interlinkages across disciplines. They understand that concepts, principles, laws and theories cannot be viewed as isolated parts, but together contribute to a holistic understanding of the world.
e. *Developing an understanding of the relationship between science, technology, and society*: Students appreciate the contribution of science to society, and how different societal needs led to the generation of scientific knowledge. They develop an understanding of issues related to connections between science, technology, and society, including the ethical aspects and implications.
f. *Developing a scientific temper*: Students develop critical and evidence-based thinking, and freedom from fear and prejudice. They develop curiosity, a sense of aesthetics, and creativity in science. They imbibe scientific values and dispositions – honesty, integrity, scepticism, objectivity, tenacity, perseverance, collaboration and cooperation, concern for life, preservation of the environment.

A major challenge related to science in the school curriculum is neglect of the development of conceptual understanding and the process capacities of doing science.

a. Science teaching-learning is mostly based on the textbook, with the focus on facts and definitions. One reason for this is the curricular load, which reduces the time available for exploration and discussion. The development of conceptual understanding and process capacities requires time, which is currently missing. The process of inquiry, central to learning science, requires some flexibility with respect to time. However, schools have a rigid timetable.
b. Another challenge is the disconnect between what students observe and experience outside school, and the school curriculum. Students come to school with their own theories about the world around them. These theories develop as they observe the things/environment around them and seek explanations for what they see. Often, these theories conflict with what is being discussed in the classroom. Their existing notions do not get addressed in the classroom, and there is a separation between 'home' and 'school' science.

c. As students move to higher grades, the demands on them increase, and the curricular load becomes greater. The need for abstract thinking also increases. It is critical that the students develop the capacities to be able to make the progression. However, the current focus on facts does not build these capacities. Also, the time for understanding each concept is limited, so alternative conceptions may develop that are difficult to address. Even when events like science fest, Baal Vigyan, science exhibitions, etc. are organized, the focus is on theoretical understanding rather than problem solving or discovery.
d. While lack of infrastructure is common across curricular areas, learning science especially requires access to apparatus, equipment, and laboratories. Unfortunately, this is a neglected area. Low cost, easily available materials are also not used since teachers lack the capacity to identify what is needed and how to develop it. At the Secondary Stage, access to a laboratory is non-negotiable – students must be able to manipulate apparatus, use materials and design simple experiments to truly develop important competencies related to science.

Curricular Goals, Competencies and Illustrative Learning Outcomes at Secondary Stage

Curricular Goals 1

Explores the world of matter, its interactions, and properties at the atomic level.

Competency 1.1 Describes classification of elements in the Periodic Table, and explains how compounds (including carbon compounds) are formed based on atomic structure (Bohr's model) and properties (valency)

Competency 1.2 Investigates the nature and properties of chemical substances (distillation, crystallization, chromatography, types and properties of mixtures, solutions, colloids, and suspensions)

Competency 1.3 Describes and represents chemical interactions and changes using symbols and chemical equations (acid and base, metal, and non-metal, reversible and irreversible)

Curricular Goals 2

Explores the physical world around us, and understands scientific principles and laws based on observations and analysis.

Competency 2.1 Applies Newton's laws to explain the effect of forces (change in state of motion – displacement and direction, velocity and acceleration, uniform circular motion, acceleration due to gravity), and analyses graphical and mathematical representations of motion in one dimension.

Competency 2.2 Explains the relationship between mass and weight using universal law of gravitation and connect it to laws of motion.

Competency 2.3 Manipulates the position of object and properties of lenses (focus, centre of curvature) to observe image characteristics and correspondence with a ray diagram, and extends this understanding to a combination of lenses (telescope, microscope)

Competency 2.4 Manipulates and analyses different characteristics of the circuit (current, voltage, resistance) and mathematize their relationship (Ohm's law), and applies it to everyday usage (electricity bill, short circuit, and safety measures).

Competency 2.5 Defines work in scientific terms, and represents the relationship between potential and kinetic energy (conservation of energy) in mathematical expressions.

Competency 2.6 Demonstrates the principle of mechanical advantage by constructing simple machines (system of levers and pulleys).

Competency 2.7 Describes the origin and properties of sound (wavelength, frequency, amplitude), and differences in what we hear as it propagates through different instruments.

Curricular Goals 3

Explores the structure and function of the living world at the cellular level.

Competency 3.1 Explains the role of cellular components (nucleus, mitochondria, endoplasmic reticulum, vacuoles, chloroplast, cell wall), including the semi permeability of cell membrane in making cell the structural basis of living organisms and functional basis of life processes.

Competency 3.2 Analyses similarities and differences in the life processes associated with nutrition, reproduction, and transport of materials in organisms (transport of water and photosynthesis in plants; digestion, circulation, breathing and excretion in animals; absorption of nutrients in fungi).

Competency 3.3 Describes cellular mechanisms of heredity (DNA, genes, chromosomes), variation and diversity (changes in sequence of DNA, movement of organisms carrying alleles in the population).

Curricular Goals 4

Explores interconnectedness between organisms and their environment.

Competency-4.1 Applies the knowledge of diversity at the cellular level and the ecological role organisms play for the classification of living organisms (five-kingdom classification; autotrophic, heterotrophic nutrition; prey, predator, and parasite).

Competency-4.2 Illustrates different levels of organisations of living organisms (from molecules to organisms).

Competency-4.3 Analyses different levels of biological organization from organisms to ecosystems and biomes, and interactions that take place at each level.

Competency-4.4 Analyses patterns of inheritance of traits in terms of Mendel's laws and its consequences at a population level (using models and/or simulations).

Competency-4.5 Analyse evidence demonstrating the consequences of the process of natural selection on biological evolution in terms of changes – structure, and function of organisms.

Curricular Goals 5

Draws linkages between scientific knowledge and knowledge across other curricular areas.

Competency-5.1 Analyses and communicates views on the impact of science and technology on human life through various modes (essay, poster, play, story, presentation, picture book, cartoons, graphic novel).

Competency-5.2 Examines a case study related to the use of science in human life from the perspective of social sciences and ethics (e.g., Marie Curie, Jenner, treatment of patients with mental illness, the story of the atomic bomb, green revolution and GMOs, conservation of biodiversity)

Competency-5.3 Applies scientific principles to explain phenomena in other subjects (sound pitch, octave, and amplitude in music; use of muscles in dance form and sports)

Curricular Goals 6

Explores knowledge in India and its connection to scientific ideas.

Competency-6.1 Describes indigenous practices related to health and medicinal herbs.

Competency-6.2 Describes the empirical evidence used in Indian medical practices (Ayurveda, Unani) and astronomy (Aryabhata's and Varahamihira's contributions to astronomy).

Competency-6.3 Identifies contributions of Indian thought to scientific ideas (atom, sound, material properties, metallurgy, chemical reactions, motion of bodies, estimations at astronomical scales).

Curricular Goals 7

Explores the nature of science by doing science.

Competency-7.1 Develops accurate and appropriate models (including geometric, mathematical, graphical) to represent real-life events and phenomena using scientific principles, and use these models to manipulate variables and predict results.

Competency-7.2 Designs and implements a plan for scientific inquiry (formulates hypotheses, makes predictions, identifies variables, accurately uses scientific instruments, represents data – primary and secondary – in multiple modes, draws inferences based on data and understanding of scientific concepts, theories, laws, and principles, communicates findings using scientific terminology)

Science Education and Science Textbook at Secondary Level as per NEP 2020

The importance of science in the scheme of general education for school children can scarcely be over-emphasized. The Kothari Commission (1964-66), The Education Policy Resolution (1968) and the "Curriculum for the Ten-Years School – A Framework" prepared by the NCERT (1975) have all recommended that highest priority be given to the teaching of science, mathematics and languages at the school stage. The national policy of education, 1986 (NPE) emphasized to strengthen the programmes of science education. It inculcates well defined abilities, problem-solving, decision-making skills in the child and to explore the correlation of science with health, agriculture, industry and other exposures of daily life. Inculcation of scientific temper is one of the items constituting core curriculum in the NPE (1986).

According to NPE (1986) science teaching should not be merely emphasized explanation of scientific concepts but also the experience of child with his environment. The students have the opportunity to care scientific apparatus and execute the experiment appropriately by following proper procedure with respect to theory and principles of science. Therefore, adequate laboratory facilities should be provided in all schools. A library having sufficient number of reference books of science should be provided in all the secondary and higher secondary schools. It is, therefore, essential that adequate laboratory demonstration facilities should be available in all schools. A good library, having sufficient reference books and supplementary readers on various science subjects is necessary for all secondary and higher secondary schools. However, according to the available information, a large number of schools in the country do not have adequate laboratory facilities with the results that teaching of science in schools is unsatisfactory.

Generally, in our educational system some common subjects are included for basic knowledge in addition to that there must be emphasized to the student's choice and flexibility. Science teaching and examinations are always keeping the students in a well versed and planned way to make it fruitful, and it produces good number of scientists and helps their families, nation at large and ultimately great flexibility will be offered for remaining courses. This enables the students to be well equipped for making them future scientist and gives enormous knowledge through various media and newspapers to get acceptance by the future generation for maintaining continuation of studies for acquisition of scientific knowledge. The students and teachers make the science class to be a best educational platform where both participate and be well convinced, solving all reasonings in a scientific method and the total curriculum in science as well as other subjects to envisage easy stigmas of the studies like analytical, logical, rational and qualitative thinking.

National Textbooks with Local Content and Flavour

NEP 2020 suggests that more emphasis is given to the content of school curriculum on constructivist approach rather than rote learning. All the Science Textbooks published nationally must be modified according to the need and suitability of local context. To make the Science Textbook, both teachers and students, if required, may change according to the Regional Concepts. The foremost aim to produce a good and well-versed textbook is to maintain economical values as well as user friendly educational system. To make the Science Textbooks error free and genuine with an affordable price and the syllabus as prescribed in the guidelines by Education Department of Centre and State, the participation of NCERT, SCERT, public private partnerships, scholars and experts is required.

In the light of National Education Policy 2020 it is not merely factual knowledge of scientific matters that is important but the cultivation of scientific outlook and scientific temper –qualities which have significance beyond the domain of science literacy. If the science teacher does not consciously help to develop the scientific temper and the student has not even a suspicion of what it means, if they go on playing or toiling at physics and chemistry or biology but cultivate no objectivity of scientific outlook or scientific integrity to my way of thinking in the deeper educational sense, they are just wasting their time. In science education, the main issue has been the large gap that separates the curricular objectives and their implementation through syllabus, textbooks, classroom practices and examinations. It is imperative to address these concerns and formulate broad strategies so that the curriculum reforms do not simply remain 'on paper' but actually benefit the school system.

Importance of Textbooks in Science Education as per NEP 2020

As a role of information source, the knowledge presented in the textbooks and used by one particular generation represents the knowledge that society wants to transmit to its children to prepare them for life as worthwhile members of that society (Pingel, 1999). Textbooks also organize scientific knowledge and science as a discipline (Olesko, 2006). Therefore, textbooks from previous generations are sources of information on changes in science teaching and the bigger issue of the prevailing scientific paradigm described by Kuhn, referred to in (Guisasola et al., 2005; Clericuzio, 2006). Although some researchers see text as a mere vehicle that delivers its content without influencing learning (Clark, 2001), but most researchers recognize the facilitator function of the textbook (Ogan-Bekiroglu, 2007).

Since learning is an active constructive process involving its interaction with the textbook, the characteristics of a specific medium must influence the learning process (Johnsen, 1993: Kozma, 2001). What the students actually learn from textbooks is mediated by the school context (teacher, peers, instruction, assignments) (Mesa, 2004). In their role as facilitators, textbooks can be used with a wide range of activities, ranging from individual to group activities and from lectures to inquiries (House, 2000); from introductory activities to application practice (Franssen, 1989).

The textbook's role as facilitator can extend the learning opportunities from the classroom where the teacher acts as facilitator, to the home where quality printed material can facilitate learning and guide learners through appropriate learning activities

(Ogan-Bekiroglu, 2007) and even direct them to resources in their own environments. According to Reddy (2005), textbooks are especially valuable to poorer communities where the school and textbooks are the only resources accessible to most learners.

A textbook can be a book or a device divided into a set of study aids, consisting of a textbook, workbook and teacher's handbook (Pingel, 1999; Sitte, 1999: Mikk, 2000). Each of these fulfils the specific purpose of textbook. Apart from textbooks, workbooks are prepared to contain assessment and exercises questions and provide appropriate spaces to answer the questions. When the learner gives the answers to questions in a single traditional textbook, they have to give answers in different books. It is very tedious to refer to both books. Some teachers prefer to use separate workbooks. This is only a practical arrangement and the questions must be developed and considered as integral part of the textbook (Nazarova & Gospodarik, 2006). As learning methods or textbook writing conventions improve, more efficient textbooks can be composed (Mikk, 2000).

Importance of Biological Science at Secondary Level

There are two main branches of natural sciences, physical sciences and life or biological sciences. Physical science studies different aspects of non-living matter in the nature. It includes Physics, Chemistry, Geology etc. Biological science includes the study of living matter and organisms. It is divided into Zoology and Botany. Thus, biological science is the term used for such sciences or subjects of learning which help in understanding and knowing life, living components and living things.

On the basis of recommendations of Kothari Commission, biological sciences have acquired a prestigious and suitable place in school curriculum. Biology has made tremendous progress in recent years. The theories of Charles Darwin and Thomas Henry Halsey have established the evolutionary principles of Biology, the simple but useful experiments of Gregor Johan Mendel formed the basis of modern genetics and the momentous finding of DNA by James Watson and Francis Crick gave us insight into the mystery of the basic process of life itself. Research in Biological Science and their implications play an important role in improving methods and materials. It assists the teacher in the construction of effective teaching-learning process. A textbook includes organization of the content, pictures, examples, visuals and exercise. Biological science has been prepared by the Board of Secondary Education, Odisha in collaboration with State Council of Educational Research and Training, Odisha. Both the institutions are responsible and accountable for teaching students at secondary stage in Odisha. Under all these objectives again various specific behavioural changes can be spelled out based upon the nature of lessons of physical and life sciences.

Criteria of Quality Biological Science Textbook

The quality of science textbook followed didactic principles and it should incorporate the content in efficient manner of the principle. The most important criteria for a good science textbook is that it should cover the understanding level of students and experience with previous level science concepts. While writing the Biological Science Textbook following four specific criteria must be followed.

I. *General Criteria*: The structure is crystal clear, technical support is considered, the content learning is goals oriented. The textbook's content is coherent with educational programme. The inductive approach is used, and the content is correct.
II. *Textual Character:* Text is linguistically correct and appropriate. Text contains motivational elements; text encourages active learning and text contains activities at different cognitive levels.
III. *Pictorial Criteria*: Visuals are of high quality; visuals contain motivational elements. Visuals stimulate recall, meaning that pictorial material must include information to elicit student's prior knowledge so that new information can foster new comprehension of a new concept, integration of visuals and texts, pictorial material must be explained with textual elements and different types of visuals, images, photographs, drawings, conventional – images like graphs, diagrams are used and stimulate higher-order cognitive processes while learning science concepts.

Evaluating Science Textbooks – Theoretical Framework

Textbooks are the most significant ways for teaching. It is important both for teachers as well as students and it should be effectively used by both. An effective science textbook is divided into three parts. The initial part is the content section. It provides the overall details of the entire textbook. The reader can get a bird's eye view of the whole book before going into the details of the book. The second part consists of lessons. These lessons are constructed by scientific facts made of illustrations, diagrams and other such presentations. It is also added with various activities, examples, etc. After each lesson there are exercises, suggestions for auxiliary experiments, technical terminology. In some lessons, life history of great scientists with their historical background is also given. Each lesson is sequentially arranged with psychological principles and is closely linked with age, abilities and interests of the students.

The third part of the textbook ends with bibliography and sometimes with a glossary. The textbook is meant for general and intensive study. Thus, the students should be motivated by the textbook for intensive learning. It is less expensive as compared to other means of learning like film strips, films or videos and it should motivate the students with individualized instruction. They should learn from the textbook as per their own pace and abilities. It facilitates learning in such a way that students can organize their learning experience in a better way.

It also helps the teachers to develop their skill in planning and presenting the content in an organized way. He/ she can present the content of the book with a variety of meaningful learning experience. The mechanical makeup and appearance of the textbook also plays a significant role in attracting the students to study. The artwork of the cover page, its size, the quality of paper, the printing of letter size, printing of illustrations, headings and sub headings of the lessons, space between the lines, printing of back page and binding contribute significantly towards the quality of the textbook. It should not create any inconvenience in reading. Printing should be clear, impressive and correct and the price of the textbook should be within the reach of all categories of students.

There are various procedures adopted in different states of India for selection of textbook. All these procedures are adopted to review the textbook as published by Government of India, Ministry of Education and scientific research by the name of textbook selection procedure in India.

The other method of evaluating textbook is score card method of evaluating textbook. In this method score cards should be constructed in order to make its evaluation more objective. The teacher can allot marks or scores to different aspects of the book, the following two types of score cards are used for evaluating science textbook.

1) Hunter George Score Card

Table 1.1: *Different Aspects and Marks of the Hunter Score Card*

Sl. No.	*Particulars*	*Scores*
1	Academic level of the writer	50
2	Mechanical appearance and cost	100
3	Psychological suitability	300
4	Content	250
5	Literary style	110
6	Learning activities	140
7	Help the teacher	50
	Total	1000

2) Another method is Vogel's spot check textbook evaluation scale, it is more intensive. In it, each point is assigned two marks in all sections and the total scores are to be calculated.

Vogel's spot check textbook evaluation scale (Maheshwari, 2014) follows the following criteria like, author, publisher, edition, cost, and scores. The sub part of the criteria is academic qualification of the author, organization and content, presentation of material, accuracy, readability, adjustment, teaching aids, illustration and appearance.

Another way of evaluating a textbook is presented by Collette Chiappetta (1998). These are title of the textbook, author, publisher, year of publication and cost. One of the five scores is given on the following points: One: poor, Two: weak, Three: normal, Four: good and Five: very good. A good science textbook should possess all the following features which were laid down by Thurber and Collette as listed below:

A) *Content:* Contents in the science textbook should be appropriate for the age level of the pupils. The contents in the book should be neither too easy nor too complex. The contents in the book should be according to students' needs and interests. The content in the book must be accurate.

B) *Organization***:** Content page should be informative. Indexing should be proper and covering the whole syllabus and subject matter presented should follow simple to complex pattern. The units in the textbook should be of students' interest and their usage in day-to-day life. While introducing any new concept/ topic/ idea/ theme, an inductive approach should be followed wherever possible. Language should be simple while writing textbooks. Use of ambiguous language should be avoided to the maximum extent possible. Complex sentences should be avoided, and the focus should be on simple and compound sentences. Activities should be provided at the end of each chapter. There should be a correlation between the activities and the contents covered in the book. At the end of the lesson, diversified questions (mixed type of questions) should be included like one word substitution, matching type, fill in the blank type, very short answer type, short answer type, long answer type, puzzles, true false, multiple choice, suggestions for further readings, extended learning activities, numerical questions, and if necessary, assessment for practical skills. Such types of exercises will be helpful for self-assessment and application to life situations. Glossary of the technical terms should be there at the end of the chapter. Summary should be precise and informative. Cross-curricular integration should be kept in mind. Examples presented in the book should be drawn from the local environment. The contents in the book should be free from material which is offensive to any country, culture, region, religion, language and caste or others. Headings and sub-headings should be written in bold so that they can catch the reader's eye easily. Important concepts, principles, laws and terms should be written in italics and should be underlined. All science textbooks should consist of laboratory manuals. Teacher's handbook should also be there.

C) *Literary style and vocabulary of textbook*: Literary style has more relevance to readability of the book. Following points should be kept in mind while formulating literary style: length of the sentences, number of ideas per unit, use of lead sentences or paragraphs and continuity of thought.

D) *Illustrations:* Quality and quantity of the illustrations should be kept in mind while formulating science textbooks and moreover the focus should be on the following points as well: photographs used should be neat, clean, appropriate and concept centric; diagrams should be sufficient and attractive and labelled; graphs, tables, maps and charts should be adequate; colour scheme used for different pictures should be appropriate and appealing.

E) *Mechanical make-up and appearance*: Cover page should be artistic and attractive. Picture(s) displayed on the cover page should be appropriate and according to the mental age of the students. Binding of the book should be of durable nature and should be securely bound. Length and breadth (size) should be appropriate. Paper used for the book should be of a good quality. Font size used should be readable by all ages. The layout and design of the book should be appealing. The colour scheme used in the book should be eye catching. Line spacing should be sufficient. The price of the book should not be a burden on the pocket.

F) *Authorship:* Subject centric persons should be allowed to become authors of science textbooks having experience of teaching the subject, more over having understood the actual learning situations. There must be a pre-requisite educational qualification for such authors. Most importantly, it will be better if some sort of training is given to them before becoming the authors.

Strengths and Weaknesses of Biological Science Textbook

The opinion of biological science teachers collected regarding the quality of Biological Science Textbook with its strengths and weaknesses on following aspects.

1. Academic aspect covers cover page, back page, printing quality, size of the book, quality of the paper, letter size, illustrations, picture quality, cost of the book, availability of book, binding, any defects and any suggestion.
2. Content, selection of topic, content organization, unit distribution, content presentation, naming of topic and subtopic, sequential arrangement of content, definition, language used, objectives, pictures, figures, graphs etc., experiments, explanation and discussion, activities suggested, role of laboratory, evaluation and exercises, glossary, references, websites, students' workbook, teachers' guide, any defects and any suggestions.

Role of Teachers in Textbook Evaluation

The teachers are the key personnel for choosing the best textbook for the learners with understanding of their mentality. They are giving guidelines to their students to learn fast and effectively. Although some teachers function well without the use of textbooks, studies worldwide show that textbooks are routinely used in classes (Kesidou & Roseman, 2002; Pepin & Haggerty, 2003; Ogan-Bekiroglu, 2007; Lemmer, Edwards & Rapule, 2008) and the majority of teachers use textbooks in their planning and presentation of instruction (Klassen, 2006: Arriassecq & Greca, 2007). Some teachers even use a variety of textbooks to provide them with examples of high-quality teaching strategies, activities and assessment tasks (Pepin & Haggerty, 2003; Izsak & Sherin, 2003: Henson, 2004; Newton & Newton, 2006).

The quality of textbooks is, however, more important when used by inexperienced or under-qualified teachers who follow these rigidly (Van den Berg, 2004; Ogan-Bekiroglu, 2007). Mahfoodh and Bhanegaonkar (2013) mention the role of teachers in the curriculum and assert that teachers are the key factor in the effective implementation of changes in curriculum and particularly in the textbook. Ahmadi and Derakhshan (2016) mention that teachers in their positions are able to monitor, assess and administer the education programme in particular teaching textbooks.

Bhanegaonkar and Mahfoodh (2013) define the role of teacher in curriculum and assert that "teachers are a key factor in the successful implementation of curriculum changes and particularly in textbook study". All educators are equipped for making, executing, and surveying their own educational plans and see themselves as having essential obligation regarding all of the previously mentioned obligations (Nunan, 1987). Some of them feel that trained professionals and government authorities ought to lay out educational programmes, and they feel that they are being approached to perform exercises for which they are not qualified as expected (p. 8). Educators are equipped for surveying, and regulating the instructive programme, especially reading material.

As indicated by Cunningsworth (1995), examining the perspectives of course reading clients is fundamental for the assessment of the

Table 1.2: *Examples of Studies that Measured the Use of Textbooks*

Sl. No.	*Name of the Country*	*Research on textbook use*
1.	USA	• 96% of grade 9–12 science classes use published textbooks. • 59% of a national sampling of science teachers said that textbooks had a major influence on their teaching (NSTA, 2003).
2.	France	• Teachers use textbooks almost all the time (Pepin and Haggerty, 2003).
3.	Germany	• 70% of teachers used mostly textbooks. • 20% of teachers used textbooks often. • 8% of teachers seldom used textbooks. • 2% of teachers never used textbooks (Sitte, 1999).
4.	Austria	• Textbooks are the most used teaching aid. • Textbooks were used in 87%, and in 4% of the cases teaching aids were used (Sitte, 1999).
5.	Spain	• 92% of teachers use textbooks as basic reference for planning (Huber and Moore, 2001).

Source: The Assessment of Science Textbooks (Sarita Swanepoel, 2010)

reading material. Students and teachers are the essential clients of reading material, so it is vital to accumulate and assess their input.

As per Ansari and Babaii (2002), educators are responsible for exploring textbook assessment of informative materials a fundamental part of an instructor's work. The chance exists for experienced educators to examine and give an account of the deficiencies of the course readings they use in unambiguous classes. It very well may be useful for course book writers, unpractised instructors, and prospectus fashioners. After all the analysis the textbook can be evaluated at three levels. The Figure 1.2 gives a clear understanding about the textbook evaluation criteria. The Figure is an extract from the evaluation criteria of the U.S. Department of Education expert panel on mathematics and science education, with the relevant indicators. The figure given below is developed by the researcher for evaluation of Biological Science Textbook.

	Level-1	*Level-2*	*Level-3*
Textbook	**Content**	**Outcomes**	**Explicit**
		Accuracy	All?
			Integrate?
			Facts correct?
			Relevant?
			Range?
	Layout	**Structure**	Consistent structure?
			Contents?
			Index?
			Cross-references
		Linguistic	Level correct?
			Readability
			Terminology
		Technical	Physical quality
			Typography
			Use of colour
	Didactics	**Pedagogic**	Differentiating
			Pre-knowledge
			Context
		Practical	Activities?
			Exercises
			Group work?
		Auxiliary	Tables?
			Diagrams?
			Pictures relevant?

Figure 1.2: *Criteria and Categories used by the MEAS for Evaluation of Textbook*

Source: (Astleitner, 2003)

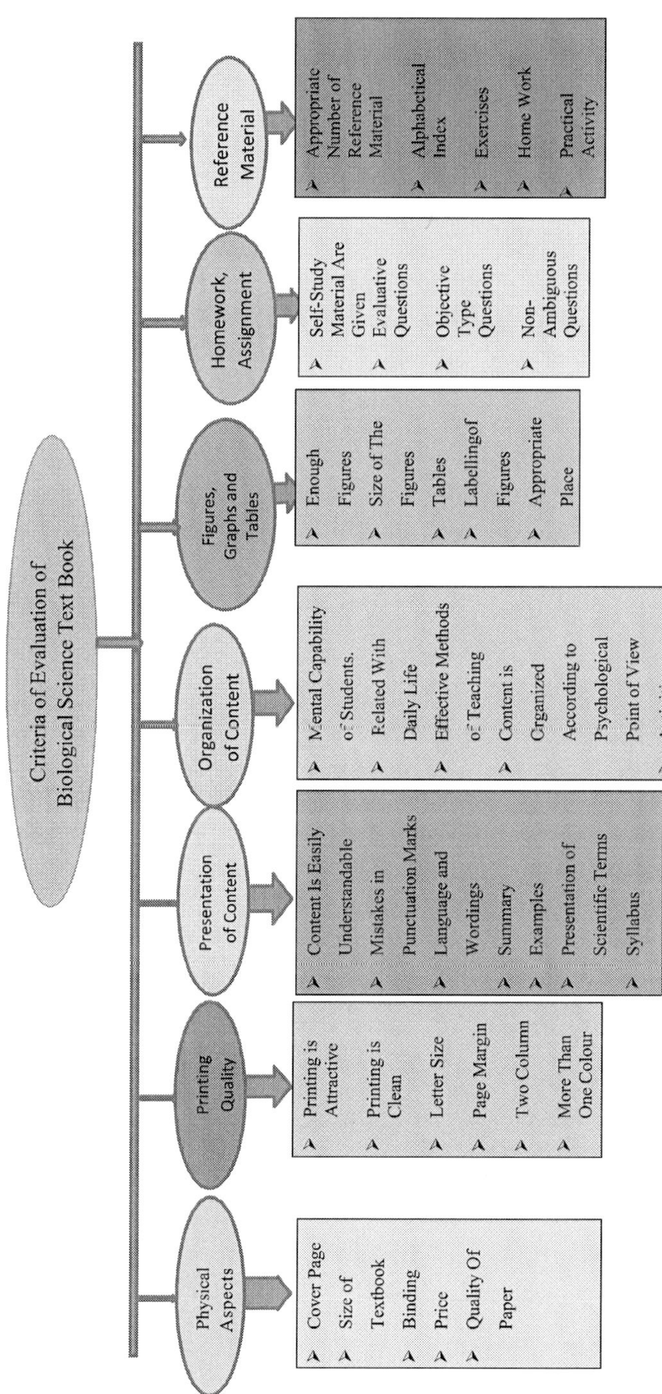

Figure 1.3 *Criteria of Evaluation of Textbook*

Need and Significance

Science education plays a significant role in secondary school stage. The Kothari Commission (1964), the Education Policy (1968), Education Policy (1986) and Programme of Action (1992) all have emphasized the need to strengthen Science Education Programme. Science Education enables the learners to acquire problem-solving and decision-making skills and to discover the relationship with health, agriculture, industry and other aspects of daily life. Inculcation of scientific temper is one of the items of core curriculum in NPE (1986). It highlights that ample opportunities should be provided to handle scientific apparatus and to perform experiments in order that the understanding of theory be reinforced through demonstration and experimentation. Scientific methods will be incorporated to inculcate scientific temper and evidence-based thinking throughout the science curriculum.

NCF 2005 defines science as a dynamic, expanding body of knowledge, covering ever-new domain of experience. In a progressive forward-looking society, science can play a truly liberating role, helping people escape from the vision poverty, ignorance and superstition. The new discoveries, inventions in science with the help of technology should be the bone of science education in schools. The content, process, language and pedagogical practices of the science curriculum should be age appropriate and should be within the cognitive reach of the learner. Science education should enable the learner to know the facts and principles of science and its application acquires the skills of 21st century like observational skill, experimental skill, problem solving and to understand the perspective of relating environment (natural environment, artifacts and people) local as well as global and appreciate the issues at interface of science, technology and society.

The NEP 2020 emphasizes on flexibility in school curriculum so and more emphasis on constructivist approach rather than rote learning in all textbooks including science. Textbooks shall aim to contain the essential core material (together with discussion, analysis, examples and application) deemed important on a national level as well as with local contexts and needs. To accomplish the aims and objectives of science education as envisioned by NEP 2020, we require certain minimum infrastructure. Currently the infrastructure facilities are grossly inadequate in a great majority of schools. The facilities need to be prominently more advanced for the secondary and senior secondary stages, with well-planned laboratories, preferably Internet and multimedia facilities and a well-stocked library containing professional development literature for teachers and career corner for students. If the required facilities are not immediately possible in all schools, they must be available at least at the science resource centers and in mobile laboratories at the cluster, block and district levels. Local talent like electricians, lab technicians should be used in science teaching for demonstration purposes. The theoretical science paper for examinations including the Class X and Class XII Board examinations should have carefully designed experiment/technology-based questions, questions testing critical understanding and ability to solve problems. The system should display the courage of conviction to mobilize required resources to put in place support systems that will help disadvantaged children to overcome their inadequacies in learning science in a meaningful manner. The curriculum should strive to make the contribution of women to the field of science and technology 'visible'.

Teachers should be sensitized to promote equitable classroom practices to ensure science experiences of comparable quality to girls. NEP 2020 strongly recommends that research in science education should be promoted to develop the scientific temper. What are the basic ingredients of scientific temper? How can it be assessed accurately? Which strategies are most appropriate to inculcate the spirit of science in the students? Research in science education awaits answers to these questions.

At the conclusion, some of the recommendations of New Education Policy 2020 if implemented in letter and spirit in our state will result in reorientation of Science Education in our state as per global standards. These recommendations are provision of multiple exit and entry points; focus on learning outcomes, pedagogical innovations; creation of quality digital resource bank in science education in open access mode to address the issue of equity; creating autonomous science institutions free from red-tapism, international collaboration; redesigning board exams to assess conceptual clarity; focus on formative assessment with feedback; inter-disciplinary approach; making science education value-based;

science curriculum restructuring as per global standards, curriculum flexibility and focus on creativity and innovations.

The above analysis assume high quality textbooks would be prepared by NCERT and later state specific curriculum framework should be prepared, and it should be reflected in preparation of all textbooks. In Odisha, all the textbooks have been prepared by emphasizing all suggested by NCF 2005 and State Curriculum Framework (2007) characteristics by SCERT and Board of Secondary Education, Odisha. Based on NCF 2005, State Curriculum Framework 2007 focusses on:

- Linking the knowledge with outer environment.
- Getting rid of rote learning.
- Not to confer learners only to textbook but all-round development of child is emphasized.
- Evaluation should be flexible and integrated curriculum with life.
- Nurturing an over-riding identity informed caring concern with the democratic policy of the country.

Being academic authority of the state SCERT prepares syllabus as well as textbook for all Classes from I to IX. In any type of teaching learning process textbooks occupy a prominent place. Textbooks help teachers and students to get a clear picture that relating to the subject matter with respect to a particular grade or class. Textbooks are written by experienced teachers, experts and eminent authors. Teachers go through the textbooks and conduct the teaching learning activities in their respective classes. Teachers are the real practitioners in this process. Their opinion plays an important role in the whole process of classroom transaction. In the present study the opinion of biological science teachers on biological textbook of Class IX have been taken. After NCF 2005 and 2007 the Biological Science Textbook has been prepared but till now no revision has been done in this regard; so far review of related literature has been done by the researcher. Here the said textbook has been analyzed chapter wise and also the opinion of teachers has been collected and analyzed to know whether the content has been prepared by as per the objectives formed by NCF 2005 and SCF 2007. Whether the various aspect of textbook are appropriate or needs improvement, what are the merits of the book and what are the demerits of the books.

Being a science teacher having 10 years of teaching experience author had an opportunity of conducting research on science teaching and evaluating the biological science textbook in significant number of schools in Odisha. The author captured some observations in her research.

The teachers had limited knowledge of educational websites on science education. They were not given any practical training in constructing low-cost improvised teaching aids on zero cost budget and the level of willingness to the use of teaching aids was found low. A significant number of science teachers did not display that vigour, enthusiasm and seriousness in attending the short-term orientation/ refresher courses on training science teachers. Barring some exceptions resource persons in these training programmes had nothing new to offer. Lack of electricity in schools is one big impediment in application of technology.

Computers have been supplied to the schools without complete accessories. The investigator found that in some schools, they are being operated directly on the mains or low voltage which puts them at risk. The present study will cover all the aspects of the Biological Science Textbook of Class IX in the academic session 2019-20 prescribed by Board of Secondary Education, Odisha critically and suggest measures to improve upon it. Thus, the researcher wanted to collect the reactions of teachers and experts regarding the quality of Biological Science Textbook. This will provide a knowledge base for textbook writers, policy makers of science education. Textbook writer may benefit from the results of this investigation as they read and interpret the curriculum while writing the textbook. It will help the authority and state planners to improve the Biological Science Textbook in future. The present study has been designed to answer the following research questions.

Research Questions

1. What is the opinion of secondary school Biological Science teachers on selection of content of textbook of Class IX as per the NEP 2020?
2. What is the opinion of secondary school Biological Science teachers on various physical and academic aspects of the said textbook Class IX?
3. Whether the views of biological science teachers having teaching experience below 10 years and above 10 years vary on various aspects of Biological Science text of Class IX?
4. What is the opinion of biological science experts on various physical and academic aspects of Textbook of Class IX?

5. What are the strengths and weaknesses of Biological Science Textbook of Class IX as viewed by teachers and experts with reference to NEP 2020?
6. What are the suggestions viewed by secondary school biological science teachers and experts for the improvement of Biological Science Textbook of Class IX as per the objectives of NEP 2020?

Objectives

The present study has been undertaken with the following objectives:

1. To examine the opinion of secondary school biological science teachers on content of Biological Science Textbook of Class IX as per the objective of NEP 2020
2. To assess the opinion of secondary school biological science teachers and experts on following aspects of Biological Science Textbook of Class IX such as
   - Cover and back page
   - Printing quality
   - Getup
   - Binding
   - Cost and availability
   - Selection of topics and sub-topics
   - Presentation of content
   - Organization of content
   - Languages used
   - Diagrams, facts and figures
   - Illustrations and examples
   - Evaluations and exercises.
3. To compare the opinions of secondary school biological science teachers on physical and academic aspects of Biological Science Textbook of Class IX having teaching experience below 10 years and above 10 years
4. To find out the opinion of secondary school biological science teachers on overall assessment of Biological Science Textbook of Class IX as per NEP 2020
5. To examine the opinions of experts on various aspects of Biological Science Textbook of Class IX as per NEP 2020
6. To analyze the opinions of biological science teachers on strengths and weaknesses of Biological Science Textbook of Class IX.
7. To examine the opinions of biological science teachers and experts on their suggestions to improve the Biological Science Textbook of Class IX as per NEP 2020.

Hypothesis of the Study

1. There exists a significant difference between the opinion of secondary school science teachers having teaching experience below 10 years and above 10 years with respect to different aspects of biological science textbook of Class IX:
   (i) Physical aspects of textbook
   (ii) Printing quality of textbook
   (iii) Presentation of content
   (iv) Organization of content
   (v) Figures, graphs and tables
   (vi) Homework, assignment and self-study material
   (vii) Reference material.

Operational Definition of the Term Used

Science Textbook: Under the secondary school science curriculum in Odisha both physical and biological science have been included. In the present study the Biological Science Textbook of Class IX prescribed by Board of Secondary Education, Odisha for the academic session 2019-20 has been selected.

Secondary Teachers: Secondary school science teachers (CBZ) who are teaching biology.

Opinion: A view, judgement or appraisal in the mind about a particular matter (Marriam-webster Dictionary). In the present study, opinion of secondary school biological science teachers has been taken on various aspects of biological textbook Class IX.

Scope and Delimitation of the Study

1. The study is limited to the study of the opinion of biological science teachers on Biological Science Textbook of Class IX for the academic session 2019-20.
2. The present study has been delimited to the biological science teachers at Government Secondary Schools of Cuttack district controlled and managed by Department of School and Mass Education, Government of Odisha.
3. The study is delimited to biological science experts who are associated with preparation and evaluation of Biological Science Textbook recognized by Board of Secondary Education, Odisha.

II

Studies on Science Textbooks

Introduction

Review of the previous related studies is an essential part of any investigation as it provides the familiarity with the field in advance where the investigator would be working on. It gives the investigator a background of a problem area, clear prospective of the problem under study, helps planning the study properly and selecting or developing tool for data collection and selecting techniques for the analysis and interpretation of data. The review enriched the investigator with new understanding and insight in the concerned area leading to the present investigation.

To ensure this familiarity a review of research literature was done. It allowed the researcher to know how much amount of work has been done in the concerned area. The researcher should be aware of the previous work that have been done in the connected field so that duplication is avoided, and the researcher's work would serve useful. Review provides an overview of the literature informing the implications of findings of the research. It is divided into six main sections where the literature provides concerned critical discourse analysis, opinion editorials, ideology, languages used in editorials power and social relations are considered.

Review means reference to discussions and going through intensively into course or curriculum or the subject matters. The clarity of the problem is possible only with the thorough understanding of knowledge available in the area of research. It avoids replication and suggests the method, procedure, sources of data and statistical techniques appropriate for the solution of the problem and findings. The review of related literature provides some insight regarding strong points and limitations of the previous studies. It enabled us to improve our own investigation and to arrive at the proper perspective of the study. The studies have been analyzed by keeping objective, methodology and findings of the study in mind and to strengthen the rationale of the present research.

The review of the literature allowed the researcher :

- To Acquaint the researcher with current knowledge available in the field in which direction the research is going to be conducted by the researcher.
- To obtain a detailed knowledge of the topic being studied.
- To set an understanding of the previous necessary work.
- To avoid unnecessary replication of the work.
- To be familiar with the areas and sub-areas of research.
- To obtain the means to carry out the investigation of the study.
- To select the size and structure of the sample.
- To compare and contest and new dimensions of result.

Quite a good number of studies are available in the area of curriculum and textbook evaluation in the field of science education in India and abroad. Some of the related studies are discussed as follows.

Review of Related Studies on Textbook Analysis

A thorough and systemic literature review was done by the researcher on evaluation of textbooks on science subject in general and biological science subject in particular. Very few studies are available on opinion of biological science teachers on Biology Textbook which are given below.

Parthasarathy and Premalatha (2022) conducted a study entitled content analysis of visual representations in Biology Textbooks across selected educational boards from Asia to explore the nature of visual representations in biology textbooks across five educational boards across Asia through quantitative and qualitative content analysis. Descriptive statistics was used during the quantitative analysis. Under this newly developed typology and taxonomy (coding scheme), visuals in Biology Textbooks can be categorized into 19 different categories. The findings of the study summarized the characteristics of visual representation usage in these textbooks in terms of their prevalence, distributional differences and trends. Through this study, a new perspective on the taxonomy and classification of visual representations, especially for Biology Textbooks, has been proposed. Biology teachers and textbook authors can gain insights through the findings of the study.

Hamid et al. (2021) conducted a study to know the extent to which the science book for the sixth grade of primary school included the skills of the twenty-first century. To achieve the goal of the research, the researchers used the descriptive analytical method, represented by the method of content analysis. The content of the science book for the sixth grade was analyzed, and the researchers prepared a content analysis tool that was built in light of the twenty-first century to measure skills, and this research tool was prepared in its initial form and it included a list of twenty-first century skills, The twenty-first century skills that must be available in the science book for the sixth grade of elementary school consist of nine main skills as listed above from. The variation in the availability of twenty-first century skills in the science book for the sixth grade of primary school, where: i) the skills of critical thinking and problem solving got the highest rate, while the initiative and self-direction skills came in the second highest rate and productivity skills and accountability is ranked third at a rate the percentage of availability of innovation and creativity skills communication and cooperation skills (11.29 per cent), computing and information technology culture skills (4.4 per cent); ii) flexibility and adaptation skills (3.67 per cent); iii) social skills and understanding Multiculturalism (3.65 per cent); iv) leadership skills and responsibility (5.98 per cent). In light of the research results, the researchers recommend that the benefit from the results of the current study and develop science books in the Republic of Iraq in light of the skills of the twenty-first century and reconsider the content of science books for all educational levels in terms of their handling of the twenty-first century skills; give them their due importance in preparing the textbook.

Karel and Martin (2019) conducted a study on science education textbook research trends: a systematic literature review to find out what attention has been given to research and textbook analysis since 2000 and to follow the trends in this area which are being observed. The findings of the study showed that science textbook research represents a very wide and still evolving area. This study addressed several of the top three research topics (learning concepts, teaching, goals, policy and curriculum, philosophy, history and not otherwise specified (NOS) items. In this study, the textbook especially concerns three main topics connected with content and its conception and presentation. On the contrary, using textbook, possible problems and textbook evaluation by teachers and students are less frequently dealt with.

Silvi et al. (2019) conducted a study on integrated science textbook on the theme of tsunami by using webbed model based on a problem solving to encourage students' preparedness toward disaster. The evaluation of the validity of textbook was determined on the basis of proper quality. This study evaluated the validity of the textbook on different aspects like presentation style, content, and language and faced using Opinionnaire was developed based on Likert Scale. On account of value of V: the content, presentation style, language and face of the textbook was considered as valid. This study revealed that the textbook mostly fulfilled all the objectives of its standard quality criteria.

Kumkum and Rani (2019) conducted a study on Content Analysis of Science Textbooks. The study briefly analyzed progress in a specific area. In this study, the researcher surveyed the literature accessible on the content analysis of science textbooks from different countries. This paper investigated the major focused area of science textbook analysis in the twenty-first century, with this researcher surveyed 25 studies executed between the years 2000 to 2018. The researcher categorized the surveyed literature based on six validation criteria of the science curriculum, proposed by the National Curriculum Framework 2005. The outcomes of the study showed that the most concerned field of science textbook analysis in recent years was related to environmental and ethical issues. The available literature reviewed by the researcher also revealed most studies confirm that science textbooks failed to satisfy the real purpose of science education.

Anuradha (2019) conducted a study on evaluation of science textbook for Secondary classes as prescribed by CBSE to analyze and evaluate Science textbooks for Classes IX and X, as prescribed by CBSE in all secondary schools all over India. The research was conducted in two stages: a theoretical evaluation and an empirical evaluation. The theoretical evaluation was based on the researcher's experience, expertise, and the literature on textbook evaluation. The empirical evaluation was based on data collected from 20 teachers and 200 students at ten different secondary schools in Delhi-NCR in the form of rating scale. The evaluation sought to find out the users' views on the qualities of the textbooks, and the users' recommendations for improvement. The results suggested some areas that textbooks needed improvement regarding the more varied types of activities, project work, effective figures, illustrations and diagrams, and redesigning of cover page. The findings accentuated the need to revisit the content by textbook writers to make it more interesting and challenging.

Rebecca and Alesha (2018) executed research on "Secondary students' perceptions of open science textbooks" to examine the perceptions of middle school students who use open textbooks in place of traditional textbooks. The findings of the study were: Open textbook created by teachers in Grade 6 through 9 replaced conventional science textbooks provided by mainstream publishing companies. Therefore Grade 9 students were not included in this study. At the end of first quarter, middle school students (Grade 6 to 8) who used the open textbook were surveyed. The survey included quality area, presentation of content questions and an opportunity for students to explain their responses. There were qualitative and quantitative indications that students' perceptions of an open textbook in place of a standard textbook were improving students' attitude and behaviour and behaviours towards learning.

Students' responses to this survey were indicative that the flexibility of open textbooks was more rigid, copyright restricted textbooks typically were used in the classroom. Most of the students' responses supported the argument that the open textbook addresses both of these challenges by being readily available and modifiable to respond to the learners' needs and maintain relevance.

UNESCO (2018) on "textbook research and textbook revision" had given following findings on textbook analysis: The methods of textbook research had evolved so as to meet the needs of different analytical purposes: these included identifying the obvious content coverage, didactical approaches or uncovering the hidden curriculum, the underlying assumptions and the connotations, which a text might evoke in the student's mind. Both quantitative and qualitative methods should have been used. Quantitative methods like frequency and space analysis measure the text and determine how many times a term was used, or a person or people were mentioned and how much space was allotted to a topic. Qualitative methods such as hermeneutic analysis reveal underlying assumptions that could not be measured — what did a text tell us, what messages did it transmit. If applied which less strict methods which relied more on the reviewer's own value system and understanding of the text. There was a range of tried-and-tested software available for the computerized qualitative analysis of various types of 'text'. They could process test files, image files, audio files and video. Deductive and inductive approaches were included during preparation of textbook analysis. Linguistic investigation offered insight into how messages were characterized and transmitted, examining facts, events, persons and processes mentioned in the text, long textbook passages were often written in the passive voice. The change of paradigm was from knowledge-based education to outcome-oriented learning stresses skills and competencies rather than rote learning and memorization of facts. The methodology of the learning process influenced the content selection criteria, and the way topics were presented. Textbook was prepared by the senior teachers and experts who met the intellectual capacities of their young readers. For the preparation of good textbook an expansion of the body of textbooks writers, professionalization was needed. It could have been a challenging task for the UNESCO and the George Eckert Institute textbook network to organize such workshops for writers and reviewers of textbook alike on a regional basis to strengthen the quality of writing and improvement of textbook quality in any particular area.

Sundararaman (2018) conducted research on Grade 8 and 9 science textbooks published by the Karnataka Textbook Society, which was revised in the year 2012 based on NCF 2005. The researcher analyzed how and whether the nature of science in terms of the historical evolution of scientific concepts was presented by teachers and textbooks. The inferences of the study showed that science textbooks contained several verses in Sanskrit (also explained in English) for discussing the evolution of numerous scientific concepts. The textbook provided more examples of Indian sages which were unnecessarily included in the chapters rather than any scientific concepts. The study also revealed that the negative consequences of any invention were neglected by teachers.

Sharma (2017) studied the topic "Content analysis of Grade 6 NCERT science textbook to study the scope of developing desirable values in students" to analyze the content related to values included in Grade 6 science textbook and to study the scope of developing desirable values in students of Grade 6 through science curriculum. The findings of the study were: It revealed that the content of NCERT science textbook had many obvious and hidden values in almost all the topics which might be taught while teaching the learning process. Science subjects had a full scope of recognition of values, ideal acts of valuing moral and character educations, teacher was required to understand the hidden values in given content and find innovative methods to impart the same to students.

Mohd et al. (2017) conducted research on "Evaluation of science textbook of Class VIII of Jammu and Kashmir State Board of School Education on the basis of reactions of teachers and suggestions by experts". They evaluated the science textbook for Class VIII of Jammu and Kashmir State Board of School Education on the basis of reactions of teachers and for the science textbook for Class VIII of Jammu and Kashmir State Board of School Education on the basis of suggestions by experts. The findings of the study were: According to the teachers, most aspects of the book were up to the mark and no review but there were certain aspects of the book which needed a change such as binding of the book, size of the book and the unequal distribution of Physics, Chemistry and Biology units in the book. All these aspects needed a change so that the book could attract more and more readers towards it. According to the experts, there were few aspects in the book which needed serious change so that the book could compete at National level.

Imtiyaz et al. (2017) conducted a research on "Critical analysis of general science textbooks for inclusion of Nature of Science used at Elementary level in Khyber Pakhtunkhwa", to analyze science textbook taught at elementary level in Khyber Pakhtunkhwa province of Pakistan, to compare the general textbooks with reference to which they cover the themes for inclusion of Nature of Science and to explore the differences between the representations of the Nature of Science in science textbooks for elementary level. The findings of the study were: The analysis of books was based on validated framework of Chiappetta et al. (1991) on four themes namely, science as a body of knowledge, science as investigative nature of science, science as a way of thinking and science as interaction of science, technology and society. Findings of this study indicated that all three science textbooks of Grade 6 to 8 presented four themes but the theme "Investigative Nature of Science" had more reflection. The theme "Interaction of science, technology and society" was absolutely ignored in all three science textbooks. Therefore, the study suggested revising all three textbooks for well-balanced reflection of all the four themes in science textbooks.

Qassim and Pandey (2017) executed research on the heading "Diagrammatic representations of upper primary science textbooks based on pictorial typology" and found that upper primary level of science textbooks included less number of diagrams, and it was seen that most of them were of iconic type textbooks which depended on curriculum which was implemented in 2013. The findings of the study were: When the textbook was examined in terms of objectives in the curriculum there was inconsistency in some objectives and even though some objectives were not in curriculum, were included in textbook. The textbook was prepared in accordance with the purpose and objectives specified in the curriculum. Teachers also had similar thoughts about that it was appropriate to comply with the achievement of the book but in terms of content, teachers wanted workbook. In order to reinforce the topics learned according to the teachers' opinions needed more activity. In addition to textbooks that student's workbook was considered for inclusion. The result of the study revealed that most of the participants thought the textbook was consistent with outcomes and visual design of the book was appropriate to the student level.

Rusilowati et al. (2016) studied the topic on development of science textbook based on scientific literacy for secondary schools. The basic aim of this study was to develop scientific literacy-based science textbooks and to determine the characteristics, reliability, validity and effectiveness of the textbooks. The study initiated with product development and continued with feasibility and readability test. Data analysis was followed by percentage description and t-test. This study results in feasibility test showed that the developed literacy science textbook had average score of 90.74 per cent implying that literacy science textbook was suitable. As per the result of readability test the average score was 88.14 per cent. Implying science literacy textbook was easy to learn. The outcome of the study revealed the effectiveness of the developed science textbook was classified effective stimulant to increase students' scientific literacy.

Virginia et al. (2016) executed a study on Evaluation of a Textbook entitled "Concepts in Inorganic and Organic Chemistry" through Teacher-Users' Assessment and Students' Performance. This research envisaged on the evaluation of a textbook in chemistry. It determined the characteristics of a good textbook and it enhanced the performance of the students in chemistry. This study made use of the descriptive and quasi-experimental methods of research. The textbook was evaluated and effective in terms of layout and design, skills, language type, skills, subject and content and overall assessment. The outcomes of the study also showed a significant difference between the control and experimental groups. The students who used this textbook performed better. The book was evaluated and found to be effective in terms of the following identified characteristics: layout and design, activities, skills, language type, subject and content, and overall assessment. In order to find the results of the study also showed a significant difference between the performance of the experimental and control groups. Students who used the textbook performed better.

Ramnarain and Chanetsa (2016) executed a study on the representation of the nature of science in South African Grade 9 natural science textbooks. The analysis unveiled that textbook reflected NOS poorly, particularly, "the social dimension of science, science vs. pseudoscience, and the 'myth' of scientific method" were noted. The researcher suggested that the school science curriculum must be improved with strong emphasis that highlights the learners' understanding of scientific enterprise and development of scientific knowledge.

Mishra (2016) examined secondary level NCERT science textbooks to explore the inclusion of science, technology, environment, and Science Technology Ethics and Society (STES) issues and found that an extensive range of STES issues have been dealt with but did not have a detailed explanation and examples from the real life of the present situation. This study revealed that there was deficiency of exposure to STES issues in many chapters. Questions and answers were mostly academically oriented and questions aiming at STES issues were of little importance.

Gilavand et al. (2016) studied the components related to health education in "science textbooks of Iranian junior high school course" through content analysis. Outcomes proved that books paid the most attention to the management and prevention of diseases and the elements of "mental health". He also explored the presentation of indigenous knowledge in science textbooks to overcome the ethnic, racist, and culturally imperialist view of knowledge. He found that inclusion of an adequate number of indigenous knowledges develops a positive approach to dealing with racism, ethnicity, rooted in limited objectives of knowledge and cultural variety. The researcher recommended that indigenous people should be involved during textbook writing for the better and exact representation of indigenous knowledge helping to remove racism and imperialism.

Indumath (2016) researched and presented a paper "Who knows and does science? — Textbook analysis of Karnataka State

Board Science textbook of Classes 8 and 9" to study the ethnographic approach of the school and participants for six months and to understand how families, school, classroom, textbooks and teachers shape the experiences of learning of science and how these play a role in aspirations of students. To understand how text of science is presented and interpreted by teachers and to understand the historical development of science based on the Nature of Science framework. The findings of the study are: Using science as a medium to discuss the Hindu values and beliefs and mythical text might create a dissonance among the learners. Though it is important to discuss the culture, Indian context, contributions of the Indians to science, it is important to present the information which is authentic and verified. According to this study it was male, urban, upper caste and class who could produce and validate scientific knowledge. The rural farmers are often referred to as illiterate and ignorant and someone who need to be educated by the urban scientists as producers of scientific knowledge, various stereotypes permeate the class. Textbook writers and teachers helped to reflect and examine their own notion of science. There is a lot of scope for discussion on Nature of Science, limits of science, gender and science and interlinkages between science and society in the textbooks.

Tron (2016) conducted, "A study of science education in the secondary schools of Meghalaya" and also analyzed the science syllabus of secondary school level of Meghalaya to know the opinion of science teachers about the syllabus, superficially and compared that syllabus with CBSE science syllabus based on National Curriculum Framework (NCF 2005). The outcomes of the study showed that the objectives of science teaching-learning were not stated in Meghalaya's science teaching framework. Meghalaya Board of School Education (MBOSE) syllabus looks to be missing an important locality whereby it failed to fulfil the criteria as identified by the NCF 2005. The syllabus of Meghalaya was only fulfilling the criteria of cognitive validity and lacking in terms of content, historical, environmental, and ethical validity.

Sinan et al. (2015) presented a model on the topic "A critical analysis of Grade 5 Elementary science education textbook" to know the students attitudes comprehend the changes in the science and technology, science education textbooks should be examined and necessary adjustment should be done and to determine teacher opinions about Grade 5 science education textbook which depend on curriculum that was implemented in 2013. The findings of the study were: When the textbook was examined in terms of objectives in the curriculum there was inconsistency for some objectives and even though some objectives were not in the curriculum but they were included in textbook. Textbook was prepared in accordance with the purpose and objectives specified in the curriculum. Teachers had similar thoughts about that it was appropriate to comply with the achievement of the book but in terms of content, teachers wanted workbook. In order to reinforce the topics learned according to the teachers' opinions needed more activity. In addition to textbooks that students' workbook was considered for inclusion. The result of the study revealed that most of the participants thought the course book was consistent with outcomes and visual design of the book was appropriate to the student level.

Osama and Alhussain (2015) studied the topic "Evaluation of the Third-Class Science Textbook from the Teacher's Perspective at Madaba Municipality". This study aimed at evaluating the science textbook of the Grade 3 primary school in Jordan from the view of the opinion of teachers who followed this textbook, to find out how suitable and relevant this textbook was as per the structure of the curriculum and guidelines. As per the science teachers' opinion various aspects such as general appearance, evaluation methods contained in the book, introduction, aids and activities, the contribution of the book for the development of students' attitude towards science, number of classes in the week to the content of the book, the facilities and materials availability in the lab to carry out and the language of the book were reviewed. This study consisted of 51 teachers who were selected randomly, and the researcher prepared an Opinionnaire. The total score of teachers evaluating science textbooks of the Grade 3 was high and the percentage reached (70.6). Researcher recommended the science teachers and supervisors designing the science textbook for the development of curriculums.

Christine (2015) researched on reform guides that recommended a more authentic view of the scientific enterprise than similar text of Evaluating Junior Secondary Science Textbook Usage in Australian Schools. This study evaluated the usage of junior secondary science textbooks in Australian schools. In this study data were collected from 486 schools teaching junior secondary (years 7-10) classes, which represented all Australian states and territories through survey method. The outcomes indicated that most Australian schools used a science textbook in the junior secondary years and textbooks were used in the majority of science lessons. The textbook influencing choice was lay out, colour, illustrations and electronic technologies found in the curriculum, in addition to the textbook in junior secondary science classes. Maximum number of respondents were satisfied with the textbook; among them many were giving stress upon the subsidiary role of science textbook in the classroom. They emphasized that the textbook was one major component of teaching. A large body of research had drawn attention to the importance for engaging learning experiences in junior secondary science classes, in an attempt to attract more students into post-compulsory science courses. The reality of time and resource, and the high proportion of non-specialist science teachers teaching science, had resulted in an over reliance on more transmissive pedagogical tools, such as textbooks. Interestingly, the majority of respondents expressed high levels of satisfaction with their textbooks and many were keen to stress the subsidiary role of textbooks in the classroom, emphasizing the textbook was 'one' component of their teaching repertoire. Respondents also stressed the benefits of textbooks in supporting substitute teachers, beginning teachers, and non-specialist science teachers; who were facilitating continuity of programming and staff support in schools with high staff turnover. Implications of this study highlighted the need for high quality textbooks to support teaching and learning in Australian junior secondary science classes.

Nima et al. (2014) conducted research on the topic "A Textbook Evaluation of Socio- Cultural Contexts in Top Notch Series". The study revealed the appropriacy of socio-cultural contexts in Top-Notch Series. For this study, a survey Opinionnaire was administered to obtain opinion of 'teachers and supervisors' on describing the Series. The scope of this study revealed that the intercultural content of the series was understandable and evaluated by the participants. The textbooks had no clear objectives in the beginning and did not satisfy its objective. There was no clear consensus regarding the cultural awareness component and teachability. This study concluded some implications and suggestions for teachers and textbook designers. The respondents had taken largely a positive view of culture presentation in the textbooks. From this study it was found that textbooks in question did not satisfy teachers and supervisors expectations regarding their teachability. The important role of textbooks was in facilitating the process of teaching. The textbooks helped teachers to minimize their preparation time, cater for mixed ability students and classes of different sizes.

Garima (2014) researched on a topic "Analyzing middle grades science textbooks for their potential to promote scientific inquiry". The study investigated the 5E model of inquiry-based science learning used to analyze textbook activities for their ability to support inquiry. A proposed plan in terms of centrally placing inquiry-based tasks in curriculum organization, furthering students' engagement and role of teachers was presented. It helped in contextualizing science by means of the inquiry-based textbooks strengthening the bonds between science and society and developed critically inquiring minds in contributing to the progress of scientific pursuit throughout their lives. Inquiry-based learning required development of instruction by means of activities in which students' engagement played the crucial role. Activities needed to be truly exploratory in nature in involving students in discovering, planning and monitoring and proposing answers. NCERT textbooks have made considerable efforts to make science learning interesting to learners by integrating colourful pictures, cartoon characters such as *Bujho Paheli* by using pleasant visual imagery to make the textbook look interesting to young learner. It came forth that under same themes the textbooks were covering different topics, suggesting the distinct vision of curriculum designers about the cognitive validity of scientific content. From this study it was found that the pre-occupation with scientific principles often lead to content-oriented textbooks and teachers might skip the inquiry-oriented activities to arrive at packets of information. It was crucial to note that the way content was organized in the textbook often structured the ways in which linkages were made between different themes and grade levels.

Alaghaa et al. (2014) conducted research on the content of the Grade 2 experimental science book based on areas of creativity. The inferences of the study indicated that most attention was paid on the distribution of pictures, sentences and experiments were for convergent thinking, inadequate attention was focused on nurturing mental creativity i.e. Divergent thinking. Studies had relation with historical validity.

Morris (2014) explored the topic the interpretation of Socio-scientific issues (SSI) in the science curriculum in England. The researcher analyzed two SSI in Science textbooks focused on the genetic technology of reproduction and climatic change in detail. Analysis of the science textbook showed a distinct difference from the perspectives of social science discipline on socio-scientific issues and the approaches taken in the textbooks.

Babaei and Abdi (2014) experimented on the presence of components of emotional intelligence (EI) in textbooks of secondary school social studies and natural science. The outcomes confirmed that EI components like social awareness in texts, "self- management in the exercises, and social skill in the illustrations" were prevalent in social studies textbooks; whereas in natural science textbooks these components were not explained elaborately.

Choudhary (2014) carried out research on the status of women through food and curriculum and suggested that educational policy should focus on creating healthy and gender fairness textbooks as textbooks and curricula played a crucial role in encouraging women empowerment and also tried to overcome all kinds of gender prejudices in the curriculum. It increased gender sensitivity in students and also suggested that food culture should be the same for both men and women. In Karnataka, an exploratory and ethnographic study has been conducted by Sundaraman (2018) to evaluate classroom teaching practices, science syllabi, and textbooks to find out how it related to students' lives, contexts, and science learning settings. What types of experiences were promoted by whom, and to whom were they addressed, especially what were the experiences of girls? Class observation, analysis of textbooks, and discussion were used. Analysis of the textbook and classroom observations implied that attempts to draw the connection of science, environmental, social, and gender concerns were sporadic. There was hardly any representation of women scientists in the text.

Khineswe (2013) studied the topic "Critical analysis of science textbooks: evaluating instructional effectiveness". The findings of the study were as follows: Evaluating instructional effectiveness included contributions by authors from various backgrounds, theorists and practitioners. In analyzing science textbooks, researchers looked into the balance between theoretical and practical knowledge, the portrayal of minorities, women and gender fairness, the treatment of socio-scientific and controversial issues and the depiction of graphical information, vocabulary load, comprehensibility and readability at the intended level, the representation of indigenous knowledge, the role of textbook questions and cultural and religious sensibility. Textbooks are an important source for students to obtain knowledge. In recent years, school-based science textbooks have become similar to the web pages and science trade books with photographs, tables, textboxes, flow charts, drawings and other visual representations. The development of a new instrument and the graphical analysis protocol is based on four principles. Textbooks are an indispensable part of the educational process. It is essential that students can get accustomed to learning from good textbooks with no scientific mistakes and with up-to-date research-based approaches to learning of the subject. It is important that textbooks undergo systematic and thorough analysis using adequate and objective criteria. Textbook researchers attempt to look at the issues related to the quality of the textbook from different perspectives. The researchers evaluated the prevalent function and structure of graphics and photographs and inclusion of history of science, assessing comprehension demands and language structure, balancing gender representation and examining the textbook as a cultural object. The author observed that the contributors to this monograph have considered challenges and potentials in textbook analysis and presented their findings. It was hoped that this collective work will continue and lead to more rigorous attempts and establish a framework for analyzing science textbook in the future.

Liu and Treagust (2013) pursued research on the topic, the diagrams of secondary school science textbooks of Western Australia. The objective of the research was to observe the nature and number of diagrams in the textbook. The findings of the study revealed that "three categories of scientific diagrams (iconic, schematic, charts and graphs) have been identified and the most commonly used diagrammatic type was iconic i.e., 69.63 per cent, however schematic diagrams and charts and graphs used were 24.14 per cent and 6.24 per cent, respectively". It can be assumed that iconic pictures were easier to understand for beginners in science learning.

Qadeer (2013) conducted research on Toronto's Grade 6 textbook on electricity, to check the scientific explanation of the content and found that more sentences were "without reason-based", means maximum sentences lacked to provide reasons, why any particular thing happened. Some daily life-related examples of electricity were found, the relations between electricity and electrons were not clearly explained.

Senem (2013) executed research on the Turkish Grade 9 physics textbook to investigate the amount of presence of science process skills. The result implied that the Grade 9 physics textbook extremely included collecting and measuring data ignoring hypotheses and defined-controlling variables.

Shahmohammadi (2013) conducted research on the content of "Iranian science textbooks of elementary school to inspect the amount of attention these books pay to the motivation construct for the country's achievement". The inferences of the study revealed that Grade 3 and Grade 5 textbooks focused more on content of motivation construct than Grade 1, 2, 4 books. The most achievement motive constructs components were related to interest in continuing incomplete tasks, preservation, anticipating, and doing something well, least emphasis was on component of understanding of time, competency-based selection of friends and others.

Senem (2013) studied the Turkish Grade 9 science textbook to investigate the amount of presence of science process skills. The result showed that the Grade 9 physics textbook extremely included collecting and measuring data, however, ignoring hypotheses and defined-controlling variables

Deshmukh and Deshmukh (2011) administered research on the study titled "Textbook: A Source of Students' Misconceptions at the Secondary School Level" for Class X biology book of Maharashtra Board and Central Board. For the purpose of collection of data, the researcher conducted a test regarding misconceptions, interviewed students and analyzed some important topics of the textbooks. The consummation of this study revealed that students had misconceptions about these topics like the functioning of hearts and lungs, the difference between respiration and breathing, photosynthesis and plant respiration as these topics were undoubtedly not explained in textbooks and not clearly explained by teachers also. Interview revealed misconceptions were also found which were based on social practices. Researchers recommended that science textbook writers should reduce misconceptions because textbooks are traditionally used as reliable study material by students and teachers.

Irine and Liliana (2010) studied the topic "Biology school textbooks and their role for students' success in learning sciences" to exploring the quality of the alternative Biology textbooks in developing the students' abilities to critically analyze the textbooks they will use in the classroom and for which they will have to express alternative options in the future on the analysis of their contribution to the students' progress in the scientific knowledge and also in their personal development. The study aimed at developing some capacities of operating with a set of criteria needed in assessing the textbooks. The findings of the study were: It can be seen that the analyzed textbook of the Grade 6 obtained most of the "good" grades given to the quality aspects of the scientific content of Biology and to the interdisciplinary nature of its content. But there were also a lot of "very good" books based on the recognition of some scientific approaches at high standards. Grade 7 textbooks offered Biology knowledge that was selected and presented accurately and was relevant to the needs of the target age group. The Grade 8 textbook was of a good quality in which scientific contents were meant to eliminate the interest for other offers. The learning activities and the suggested problems only partially responded to the expectation or need of support in preparing the lessons for the future teacher-students. At the Grade 8 there was no relevant change in the assessments distribution for the didactic process of the textbook's content in comparisons to the results.

Mostafa (2010) studied the topic "The comparisons analysis of science textbooks and teacher's guide in Iran with America" which was published in the journal Science Direct Procedia (social and behavioural sciences) to know the depth of the concepts in Iranian guide book in primary school and American science anytime. The centralization of the questions and assignments in Iranian science textbook in primary school and American science anytime were in Guilford categorization. The kind of information in practical and on-practical in Iranian science textbook in primary school and American science anytime were determined. The kind of expected actions in Iranian science textbook and American science anytime were determined. The results of the researchers were unreal without noticing the cultural situation. In Iranian teacher's guide and American science anytime the knowledge and understanding were emphasized. The results of the research showed that the most contents in Iranian textbooks were concepts. But American science anytime are representing concepts and facts and in American texts the method of working was more important. Although the goals in usage level in Iranian Science Textbooks were more than American science anytime, but the teachers didn't pay attention to this fact.

So, in Iran most of the goals in the class were null curriculum. In Iran there was not any lab equipment in school. In American science anytime the outdoor activities were emphasized. American science anytime textbooks were modularly but Iranians were linear. So in Iran the teacher couldn't do any out-door activities. The questions and assignments in American science anytime were based on constructivist approach and promote the co-operative learning. The subjects in American science anytime were sensitive to the scientific changes like changes in Geology, astronomy and space, so the new materials in American science anytime is much more. In American science any time multiculturalism was attended but in Iranian text it was not pursued

Kahvei (2010) pursued a study on Turkish chemistry and science textbooks in terms of themes like gender fairness, level of questions, number of scientific vocabularies, and readability level. The outcome of this study showed that the textbooks did not provide satisfactory empirical evidence to gender equity and inquiry-based learning and the results also showed that cognitive level questions were more focused.

Elif et al. (2009) studied the topic titled "Underlining the problems in Biology textbook for 10th grades in high school education using the suggestions of practicing teachers", to determine the common misconceptions in the textbook discussed the appropriateness of the questioning techniques and examined the particular textbook according to instructional approach. The First stage: The document analysis of Grade 10 Biology textbook included subject matter content, visual material, misconceptions, question types, multidimensional questions, measurement, design of the activity, learning approach and nature of science. The textbook evaluation according to National Register of Citizens (NRC), 1990 criteria were adequate but not encyclopedic coverage, factual accuracy, incorporation of current conceptual understanding and new subject matter, logical coherence, clarity in explanation and effectiveness of illustration, appropriateness to students' level and interest and representation of Biology as an experimental subject.

In the light of findings, it became clear that during preparation of Biology textbook, National standards of science education were disregarded. The textbook was weak and inadequate as it lacked scientific research processes and questioning techniques. Then the misconceptions in the textbook made the situation even worse which could affect learning. Besides these it was emphasized by the practising teachers that the textbook encouraged students to memorize and it should be revised accordingly. In the light of these results practising teachers needed to learn the criteria as to how a textbook must be analyzed and the points to be observed in choosing a textbook, for improving the efficiency of Biology education. It was necessary to associate the information Biology with daily life. The content of the course should be well-organized so that Biology practising teachers could associate the information they acquired with their daily lives. In addition, Biology teachers were recommended to encourage the students to conduct project studies with which they could associate their information with their daily life.

Reimann (2009) carried out research on evaluating textbooks' effectiveness in presenting cultural content: Goals and outcomes, the extent to which content was used to raise cultural awareness or otherwise engage the students in a way that promoted interest and a positive understanding of the target language and relevant communities. Presentation was the way in which cultural information was included, omitted or simplified, practically how cultural content was balanced to account for immediate, short-term concerns such as teaching ability, marketability and relevance.

Bakulchanda (2009) made a critical study of science and technology textbook of Class X of Gujarat state, Jain Vishvabharati Vishvavidyalay, Ladnoo, Rajasthan (M.Ed.). The objective of the study was to study characteristic of Class X science textbook; to know opinion of teachers towards quality of science textbook; to ensure quality of graphical representation of subject matter; to evaluate overall textbook with the help of teachers; self prepared Opinionnaires were used to collect the data. The findings of the study were that Title page of textbook is attractive. Size of textbook is proper. Readability of textbook was good. Printing should have been clear and error free. Content should have been arranged according to hardness. More self-study questions should also be added.

Patel and Amrutlal (2009) a critical study of Chemistry textbook of Class XI of Gujarat state, Jain Vishvabharati Vishvavidyalay, Ladnoo, Rajasthan (M.Ed.) was made with Objectives: to study characteristic of Class XI Chemistry textbook.; to know opinion of teachers towards quality of chemistry textbook.; to ensure quality of graphical representation of subject matter; to evaluate overall textbook with help of teachers. Tools: Self prepared Opinionnaires. Findings: title page of textbook was attractive; size of textbook was proper; readability of textbook was good; printing should have been clear and error free. Content should have been arranged according to hardness. More self-study questions should have been added. More figures should have been included. Language should have been simple. More examples should have been added in every chapter.

Baraiya (2008) conducted research to evaluate the textbook of Gujarati subject of Class IX of Gujarat state. Bhavnagar University Bhavnagar (M.Ed.); to evaluate the textbook of Gujarati subject by students and teachers. The findings of the textbook were suitable for student age; there were enough pictures in textbook; enough reference books list was given in textbook; presentation and integration of content was proper in textbook; some poems from textbook could be sung; some chapters were very interesting in textbook. There were some linguistic errors found in textbook.

Prakash (2008) studied the: "A Content Analysis of Environmental Education Textbooks of Primary Stage in Schools of Rajasthan." In order to find out the extent to which the themes and sub-themes recommended by NCERT have been incorporated in textbooks of environmental studies of primary stage especially Grade 3 to 5 and second to find out the suitability of the content matter, illustration, activities and practices, exercises of environmental studies textbooks of primary stage; the third objective of the study was to suggest measures for development of existing textbooks of environmental science for primary stage and in that study it was found that 368 respondents (teachers) were selected from different government and private schools. Out of which 184 were government teachers and 184 were private primary school teachers. The outcomes of the study were: though the guidelines for the improvement of textbook were available, educationists and experts of textbooks who were assigned for writing of textbooks did not follow the guidelines. This textbook was lacking diagrams, language of the textbook was very easy in many chapters and questions provided in the textbook were mostly knowledge based. For Grade 3, number of sub-themes suggested under four themes by NCERT was 25. In the same manner 13 and 14 sub-themes were included in the textbooks of Grade 3. In the textbooks of Grade 4 and 5, sub-themes were 25 and 28 under four themes in the respective books. These textbooks lacked in diagrams, the language of the textbook was very easy in many chapters and questions of exercise were mostly knowledge based.

Rani (2008) investigated the topic of the extent of values in Class IX science textbooks of NCERT. The data were analyzed and the content using a checklist of epistemological, social, and personal values and confirmed that the values of epistemology held a prominent place in the chemistry and physics parts of the textbook, It was found that in biology, socio-cultural values were emphasized (both explicitly and implicitly). The values focused prominently in physics were "accuracy whereas in chemistry and biology it was analytical ability. From the textbook analysis, it had been found that some personal and socio-cultural values like team spirit, courage, confidence, equality, and co-operation had no place in the Class IX science textbooks, although the curriculum frameworks emphasized on them".

Miriam et al. (2008) conducted research on educators' selection and evaluation of natural sciences textbooks and highlighted the central role of textbooks in teaching and learning of science, it was imperative that textbooks provided correct content and instructional support. It was investigated that how 16 South African Grade 7 natural science educators selected their textbooks and how they evaluated these textbooks. The data were analyzed according to the constructivist paradigm and criteria found in the literature. The selection criteria that the educators listed in interviews were isolated ideas that were not designed in a constructivist framework. Recommendations were made for improvements in educator training, textbook writing and departmental guidance. Experience gained in textbook evaluation during training courses could boost educators' competence for the selection of books and detecting and compensating for their deficiencies. This study contributed to filing South African educators requiring hands-on examples which could be applied immediately in their classrooms.

Eugene et al. (2008) studied and conducted a study on "Analysis of Five High School Biology Textbooks used in the United States" for Inclusion of the Nature of Science. Five high school Biology Textbooks were examined to find the inclusion of four aspects of nature of science: (a) science as a body of knowledge, (b) science as a way of investigating, (c) science as a way of thinking, and (d) science and its interactions with technology and society. The Textbooks analyzed were Biological Sciences Curriculum Study (BSCS) Biology — A Human Approach (Kendall/Hunt), BSCS Biology — An

Ecological Approach (Kendall/Hunt), Biology – The Dynamics of Life (Glencoe), Modern Biology (Holt), and Prentice Hall Biology (Prentice Hall). The six chapters were analyzed in textbook, which were the methods of science, heredity, cell, DNA, ecology and evolution. A scoring procedure was followed with Cohen's kappa values ranging from 0.36-1.00. Five recently published Biology textbooks in the United State had a good balance of presenting Biology with respect to the four themes of science literacy used in this study than those analyzed 15 years ago, engaging students to find out answers, collecting information and learning how scientists go about their work. Hence these Biology Books incorporating national science education textbooks used in 15 years ago.

Kanaiyalal (2007) took opinion of students and teachers towards Hindi textbook at secondary level, Gujarat University, Ahmadabad (M.Ed.) to know about its acceptability and workability its strengths and weaknesses as per the requirements of students and teachers; to give suggestions to make textbook more interesting and usable. Tools: Self prepared Opinionnaires; Survey method. Findings: Content to be according to the age of students. Interesting topics need to be added. Title page of textbook was attractive. Size of textbook was proper. Readability of textbook was also good.

Hiappetta and Fillman (2007) researched on the topic of biology textbooks concerning environmental validity and found that Science and Technology Studies (STS) received less attention while presenting the nature of science. In 2013, Rashid evaluated science textbooks of Classes VIII-X of UP Board in the context of environmental awareness. The outcomes of the study showed that the textbooks had implicit inadequate quantity of facts and effects on environment. There were no appropriate explanations on environmental issues namely, Greenhouse effect or Global warming, acid rains, and ozone layer depletion, etc.

Jangaiah (2007) executed a programme on analyzing gender issues in Class VIII, IX and X textbooks of the Andhra Pradesh government as reflected in National Curriculum Forum (NCF 2005). The inferences of this study showed that gender discrimination was seen in physical and biological science books. The textual content of science textbooks contained more masculine references. Based on the outcomes, the researcher suggested that textbook authors should give equal importance to both sexes and avoid stereotyping pictures content, activities and exercises.

Chiappetta and Fillman (2007) examined "five high school biology textbooks of the U.S. to diagnose the inclusion of major dimension of the nature of science namely, science as a body of knowledge, science as a way of investigating, science as a way of thinking and science and its interactions with technology and society". The findings of the study showed that a major portion of books presents science as a body of information and textbooks frequently inspired students to investigate.

McGrath (2006) researched on Teachers' Perceptions towards the Textbooks and found their attitudes toward textbooks were based on how they used them. McGrath (2006) examined teachers' and learners' opinions toward the course books and claimed that their views and beliefs were according to the language they used, it was possible to achieve some vision into teachers' prospects of English language course books from the attitudes they used to describe them. He selected a mixture of metaphors and similes for English language course books from a course which was conducted over a two-year period, mainly in Hong Kong, contained data from two sources: (1) nearly 75 secondary school English teachers in Hong Kong, and (2) from several hundred secondary school pupils in Hong Kong. The information was collected by the teachers of those pupils. They were asked to complete the framework to know their attitudes toward the textbook. In conclusion, he concluded that it was better for the teachers to reveal their own metaphors and how these affected their use of a course book as well as the relationship between their own metaphor and those of their students.

Gilavand et al. (2006) observed the components related to health education in "science textbooks of Iranian junior high school course" through content analysis. Results proved that books paid the most attention to the management and prevention of diseases and the elements of "mental health".

Alkader (2002) conducted study on: "Analytical and Evaluative Study of the Secondary School Biology Textbooks in Yemen". The purpose of the study was: To evaluate Class XI Biology textbook for secondary schools in Yemen from teachers' perspective: To evaluate Classes X, XI and XII biology textbooks in secondary schools in Yemen: To find out if achievement of students could be improved through programmed instruction. The hypotheses of the study were that there was no significant difference in achievement of students who learned Biology "Unity of Life and Tissues" through programmed instruction method. The study was survey and experimental type. In this study samples consisted of 28 Biology teachers and 320 students for the control and experimental groups of Class XI taking biology as science subjects belonging to Education office to Sana'a city. The tools of the study were Opinionnaire for obtaining the responses of Biology teachers regarding evaluation of textbook using survey method and achievement test. The control pre-test and post-test was used in this study. The programmed texts were divided into 207 frames and each part comprised of 14 frames to be taught in one class within a period of 45 minutes with total of 15-class periods. All the data were analysed by using the frequency. The outcomes of the study were that the textbook was mainly based on memory of knowledge of facts rather than skills and attitude, the biology teachers did not appreciate the evaluation, content and elements of the Biology textbook. The textbook concentrated on cognitive aspects and it totally neglected affective and skill aspects.

RIE (2001) a study of textbooks in Biology was conducted and found that all the diagrams in the textbook could be improved and if possible, colour diagrams might be incorporated to make the book more attractive and readable. References should have been designed at the end of each chapter. Some aspects of recent advances in Botany might be given in blocks. Journals in Biology and laboratory manuals might be mentioned separately in a different book. The book should have contained teacher's guide and teachers' supportive material for better guidance. Maximum reference books in Biology might be mentioned topic-wise. The exposition of this study revealed overall reduction in size of the book from the present set-up was suggested. Cover page diagrams should have been large and distinct photographs relevant to curriculum rather than hand-drawn diagrams to be included. Size of book, thickness of paper and quality of paper should have been made better than the existing one.

Research on Teachers' Perceptions towards the Textbooks

Litz (2000) studied teachers' attitudes towards the science textbook. To this end, thirty-five EFL teachers, both male and female, with several years' of experience in teaching the series participated and the instrument to collect data which was used for the research was the Opinionnaire prepared. With respect to the results, the teachers were satisfied with the subject and the content of the series and had the same opinion that the subject and content of the textbook were realistic, interesting, challenging, motivating and relevant to students' needs. The teachers did not have very positive prospective words towards "layout and design of the series; moreover, the layout and design were inappropriate and unclear and the textbook was not organized effectively. Riassati and Zare (2010) listed some shortcomings of the textbooks: 1. Lack of supplementary teaching materials; 2. Some items and subjects within the series were not primarily based on Iranian learners' culture; 3. Some elements of series were beyond the linguistic capability of the learners; 4. Several testing exercises; 5. Series did not pay enough attention to writing skills, therefore, learners did not receive practice in this section; 6. Inappropriate number of teacher's manual. In this regard, Ahmadi and Derakhshan (2015) investigated and evaluated Iranian junior high school textbooks "Prospect 1" and its old version "RPE1". They analyzed one hundred Iranian teachers' perceptions using Razmjoo's (2010) checklist which included six criteria, namely language components, tasks, activities and exercises, language skills, teacher's manual, general consideration and critical discourse analysis features. The results of the research indicated that majority of teachers believed that Prospect1 followed CLT, and listening and speaking skills were paid more attention. In addition, grammar was completely neglected. On the contrary, RPE1 did not follow the CLT approach.

The functions textbooks could fulfil support to teachers were twofold (Reys and Reys, 2006; Russell, 1997): planning and teaching (day-to-day); and professional development (long term), in context of the educational reform process textbooks must support teachers in the translation and execution of the curriculum (Taylor, 2008a). Van den Akker (McKenney, 2001) identified three aspects of that support: a) clearer understanding of how to translate curriculum ideas into classroom practice; b) concrete foothold for execution of lessons that resembled the original intentions of the designers; and c) stimulation of reflection on one's own role, with the eventual possibility of adjusting one's own attitude toward the innovation.

Teachers' editions of textbooks could target the teachers' needs. It could provide ex-plantations of curriculum requirements, as well as the content or subject knowledge and pedagogical knowledge (Singer & Tuomi, 2003), was an example of teacher training materials that facilitated in-service training and upgrading for teachers. It was designed by the Botswana College of Distance and Open Learning for participating in sub-Sahara countries (Daniel and Menon, 2005). Mikk (2000) identified the following functions of textbooks in its support of students in their learning, motivating students to learn, represent information (transform and systemize), guiding students to acquire knowledge, guiding students to acquire learning strategies, aiding self-assessment, differentiating and facilitating value education.

Discussion of Literature Review related Science Textbook

The researcher carefully reviewed all the above studies between the years 2000 to 2022. Different kinds of study related to biological science textbook are discussed below.

Parthasarathy and Premalata (2022) analyzed the qualitative and quantitative aspects of content analysis of science textbook and concluded that the visual representation presented in the biology textbook would help the teachers to explain the concept in a more meaningful way to the learners. Hamid et al. (2021) studied the inclusion of twenty-first century skills on Grade 6 primary schools science textbook and concluded that the content of the science textbook not included all the skills of twenty-first century. Zuber et al. (2020) concluded that major portion of science textbook of Grade 8 was at concrete operational level where as a small number of contents demanded formal operational level. Karvel and Martin (2019) concluded the scope of researches on content analysis of science textbook is very wide and still evolving area. More researches in this area should be done. Kumkum and Rani (2019) highlighted that major focused area of science textbooks related to environmental issues and ethical issues and that science textbook failed to satisfy the real purpose of science education. Anuradha (2019) studied the evaluation of science textbook from both theoretical and practical aspects. The study concluded that some areas of textbooks needed improvement to include various types of activities, project work, effective figures, illustrations with diagrams and redesigning cover page. The content of textbook should be more interesting and challenging.

Rebeca and Alisha (2018) studied the perceptions of secondary school students on open science textbook in place of traditional textbook and concluded that students were in favour of open science textbook. UNESCO (2018) concluded that both qualitative and quantitative method should be adopted for textbook analysis and textbook should be written by senior teachers and experts and they should be trained professionally to work and review the textbook to meet the intellectual capacities of the learners. Sudermann (2018) concluded that science textbook should contain scientific concepts rather than verses from scientist. Whereas Mohd. F et al. (2017) concluded that science books are up to the mark and need no review as viewed by teachers and experts. However, the experts recommended for changes of layout as it was not good and well planned. Binding, size of the book should be improved. Enough emphasis has not been given on practical component of science education. Quasim and Pandey (2017) suggested that science textbook should be based on pictorial typology. Virgima S et al. (2016) concluded that science textbook was effective in terms of its layout, design, activities, skills language type subject and content and overall assessment. Whereas the study conducted by Ramurian and Choneta (2016) concluded that science curriculum must be improved with strong emphasis on the learners' understanding of scientific enterprise and development of scientific knowledge. Mishra (2016) analyzed the inclusion of science technology, environment and found that an extensive range of STES issues have been dealt with but did not have a detailed explanation. Indhumathi (2016) concluded that families, school, classrooms, textbooks and teachers shape the experiences of learning of science and those play a role in shaping the aspirations of students. Torn (2016) concluded that opinion of science teachers was not in favour of science curriculum in terms of objectives framed by NCF 2005. But Sinan et al. (2015) concluded that the objectives of textbook were not stated clearly. Sharma (2014) analyzed and concluded that NCERT textbook have made considerable efforts to make science learning interesting with colourful picture, cartoon whereas Deshmukh and Deshmukh (2011) concluded that in textbook many misconceptions like function of heart should be rectified. Study conducted by Irine, F. and Lilliana (2010) concluded that the biology science textbook obtained most of the good grades whereas the study conducted by Khoveni (2010) written textbook did not provide satisfactory empirical evidence to gender equity and inquiry based learning and focus was mostly on cognitive level of learning. Elit et al. (2009) analyzed the biology textbook concluded that it lacked encyclopedic coverage, factual accuracy, logical coherence, clarity in explanation and effectiveness of illustrations appropriateness of student level and interest. Parvesh (2006) concluded that the textbook was lacking diagrams and questions provided in the textbook were meeting the knowledge based whereas RIE Mayssor (2006) suggested that inclusion of colour diagrams makes the biology textbook more attractive readable. Reference should have been given at the end of the topic. The book should have contained teacher's guide, diagram should have been large and distinct. Size of the paper of the book and quality of the paper should be improved. Logical sequence on arrangement of topic and presentation should be improved. Litz (2000) stated in his research that teachers were satisfied with the content of the textbook. The content was realistic, interesting, challenging and motivating and relevant to student's need. The teachers have a negative view on layout and design and organization of the content.

The literature review also revealed that some foreign researchers analyzed the science textbook from more than one perspective, such as Erten, Şen and Yüzüak, 2015 (cognitive & environmental) Chiappetta and Fillman, 2007 (process, historical & environmental) and Ninnes, 2000 (historical, environmental & and ethical). In India, only Tron (2016) compared the MBOSE science syllabus with the CBSE syllabus with respect to all validity criteria. Improving the science curriculum in India also promotes improvement in textbooks. Consequently, the science textbook must meet all proposed validity criteria. Therefore, all science textbooks should be necessarily analyzed to know whether they have been written keeping in mind all the validity criteria. According to Baraiya (2008), some chapters were very interesting in textbook. There were some linguistic errors found in textbook. According to Damore (2009) all objectives of Science subject were satisfied; contents were according to age of students and more self-study questions are included. According to Suthar (2009) content should have been arranged according to hardness and more self-study questions should have been added. According to Patel (2009), more figures should have been included, language should have been simple, and more examples should have been added in every chapter. Damor (2007) in his study highlighted title page of textbook was attractive, size of textbook was proper and readability of textbook was good. The researcher had reviewed 74 studies conducted on textbook evaluation out of which 35 were Indian studies and 39 studies were conducted abroad. Similarly, out of 74 studies 32 were from science textbook evaluation, 34 were textbook evaluation in general and nine were from Bioscience textbook evaluation in particular. Further, most of the studies followed qualitative and quantitative method and other studies were survey method. All the studies were found to be significant to the present study. It is therefore strongly recommended that the textbook should be written with a perspective that promotes inquiry-based learning, understanding of the genesis of science, understanding of the natural world, understanding of issues related to science-technology society, sensitivity towards preservation of the environment, promotes positive attitude towards prejudice related to a particular area, race and religious conviction.

Research Gap

A thorough literature review was done on evaluation of textbook on science subject in general and biological science in particular. The analysis of the reviews on textbook evaluation was also analyzed in this chapter. After a thorough review researcher found that there were many studies conducted on different aspects of textbook evaluation both at national and international levels, both put the best of our knowledge, but there was not a worthwhile up to date study on perception of teachers and experts in Biological Science Textbook of Class IX. Similarly, there is no systematic study conducted on opinion of biological science teachers on quality of biological science textbook of Class IX prescribed by BSE, Odisha. Teachers play a significant role in operationalizing the textbook in classroom transaction; therefore, the present study is a humble attempt to fill the gap in the existing knowledge of research and to study the opinion of secondary school science teachers on various aspects of Biological Science Textbook of Class IX prescribed by BSE, Odisha in the academic session 2019-2020. Recently NEP 2020 is going to be implemented in our state. Hence it is necessary to conduct the research on the above topic and the output of the research will be helpful for the textbook writers and policy makers to include the findings in the development of biological science textbook as per NEP 2020.

III

Research Design and Methodology of Study

Introduction

The purpose of any research design is to provide maximum amount of information relevant to the problem under investigation at a minimum cost. Basically, research design serves two functions. First, it answers the research questions as objectively, validly and economically as possible. The research problems are usually epitomized by hypotheses. A research design suggests to the researcher how to collect data for testing these hypotheses, which variables should be treated as control variables. What method of manipulation would be more adequate in a particular context? What type of statistical analysis should be done and finally, a possible answer to the research problem, thus, a research design, after moving through the sequence of different related steps enables the researcher to draw a valid and objective answer to research problem. Second, a research design also acts as a control mechanism. In other words, it enables the researcher to control the unwanted variances. In any scientific investigation there are three types of common variances namely the experimental variance, the extraneous variance and the error variance with which the researcher is directly concerned. In this chapter, population, sample and its size, tools and statistical techniques used are presented. Research designs are an important part of research. No research studies can be undertaken without proper thinking and planning. There are many methods of collecting, analyzing and reporting research data. The decision about the method depends upon the nature of the problem and objectives to be achieved. The chapter provides a brief picture about the method, the population, the sample and the tools used in study. It also gives detail descriptions about procedure of data collection along with the statistical techniques used and the rationale underlying them. The ambit of the research is confined to a descriptive survey.

Method of Study

In the words of Hillway (1964), “to describe in detail the specific method being used, incidentally, constitutes a very good way of determining whether the method chosen has been worked out properly and is likely to prove effective. If the scholar cannot describe his method, the chances are that it is too vague and general to yield him satisfactory results."

Broudy (1963) stated that "Method refers to the formal structure of the sequence of acts commonly denoted by instruction. The term method includes both strategy and tactics of teaching and involves the choice of what is to be taught and the order in which it is to be taught".

Methods of conducting a research study vary in their nature and intent. It is the nature of the problem that determines the choice of the method to be used. The present study is an attempt to study the opinion of the secondary school science teachers and experts of Odisha about the Biological Science Book. Keeping this thing in mind, the investigator used both qualitative and quantitative approach for the study. Further, descriptive survey method was used to conduct this study.

Population

A population refers to any collection of specific groups of human being or non-human entities such as objects, educational institutions and geographical areas. A population contains a finite as well as infinite number of individuals. Population is properly defined so that there is no ambiguity as to whether a given unit belongs to the population or not. If the population is not properly defined, a researcher does not know what units to consider while selecting the sample.

Secondary Education serves as a bridge between elementary and higher education and prepares young people between the age group of 14-18 years for entry into higher education. The Directorate of Secondary Education, Odisha was set up in the year 1983 to look into Secondary Education in the State. Directorate of Secondary Education deals with administration of Government and aided Private Secondary Schools, Madrasas, Sanskrit Tolls in the State. There are 6193 government and aided Secondary Schools, 849 recognized High Schools and 151 permitted High Schools in the State. One of the major innovations in recent years has been the plans of Odisha State to set up one Odisha Adarsha Vidyalaya (OAV) (literally Odisha Model School) at each of 314 block headquarters. The Board of Secondary Education (BSE) affiliates all state schools, private schools and colleges in the state of Odisha. There are five central zonal offices of BSE, in Cuttack, Bhubaneswar, Balasore, Baripada, Berhampur and Sambalpur.

The purpose of the study is to study the opinion of secondary school biology science teachers on Biological Science Textbook of

Class IX under BSE Odisha. The study is delimited to Cuttack district only which comprises of 14 Blocks namely Athagarh, Badamba, Narasinghpur, Tigiria, Banki, Dampada, Baranga, Cuttack Sadar, Kantapada, Mahanga, Niali, Nischintakoili, Salepur, Tangi-Choudwar. Geographically, it is located at a latitude of 20-degree 03 to 20-degree 40 N and a longitude of 84-degree 58 to 86-degree 20 E. Cuttack city is flanked by Mahanadi river on the north and Kathajodi river on the south. Covering a geographical area of 3932 sq k.ms, the district is thickly populated. The district experiences a tropical climate, with the summer being hot and in the winter it is cold. As per 2011 Census, total population of the district was 2624470 which consisted of 1352760 (Male) and 1271710 (Female).

The population density of the district is 667 per Sq. km. and the Literacy Rate is 85.5 per cent. Sex ratio of the district is 940 females per 1000 males. The population of the study covers all the secondary school science teachers of Cuttack districts of Odisha. From the Table 3.1 it is revealed that the total number of secondary schools in Cuttack district is 324 whereas total number of teachers is 3666.

Table 3.1: *Block wise High Schools of Cuttack District*

S. No.	*Name of The Block*	*Number of High Schools*	*Total Number of Teachers*
1	Athgarh	17	209
2	Banki	14	284
3	Baramba	25	262
4	Baranga	11	133
5	Cuttack Sadar	16	250
6	Dampara	05	69
7	Kantapara	16	194
8	Mahanga	31	273
9	Narsinghpur	20	178
10	Niali	22	239
11	Nischintakoili	32	290
12	Salipur	27	274
13	Tangi	15	162
14	Tigiria	08	100
15	Athagarh NAC	02	25
16	Banki NAC	02	51
17	Choudwar MPL	07	82
18	Cuttack MC	38	591
19	ARC Charbatia	0	0
	Total	324	3666

Table 3.2: *Block wise Science Teachers*

S. No.	*Name of the Block*	*Number of PCM Teachers*	*Number of CBZ Teachers*	*Total*
1	Athagarh	25	16	41
2	Banki	13	14	27
3	Baramba	30	19	49
4	Baranga	11	12	23
5	Cuttack Sadar	24	26	50
6	Dompara	07	05	12
7	Kantapara	15	15	30
8	Mahanga	30	27	57
9	Narsinghpur	19	23	42
10	Niali	18	20	38
11	Nischintakoili	26	29	55
12	Salipur	29	23	52
13	Tangi	13	17	30
14	Tigiria	05	10	15
15	Athagarh NAC	04	04	08
16	Banki NAC	05	06	11
17	Choudwar MPL	07	09	16
18	Cuttack MC	67	59	126
19	ARC Charbatia	0	0	0
	Total	348	334	682

From the Table 3.2 it is found that in all blocks the total number of secondary school teachers working in secondary schools of Cuttack district is 682 out of which 348 are PCM teachers and 334 are CBZ teachers. Thus, all the Biology Science Teachers (334) working in secondary schools of Cuttack district are the population of the study.

Sample and Sampling Technique

Sampling is the basis of any scientific investigation. Since in educational research, it is neither practically expedient nor scientifically desirable to approach the total population. Therefore, the technique of sampling is employed in which instead of every unit of population being tapped only a part of population was drawn and studied.

In the study, the sample was drawn from the high school teachers and experts of Cuttack district. Due to paucity of time and money, the schools were selected on the basis of convenience. Hence, convenience sampling procedure was used for selection of schools from Cuttack district. One hundred twenty-nine (129) government high schools of Cuttack district, affiliated to BSE Odisha were selected as sample of the study. Further, a secondary school teacher

Table 3.3: *Sample Teachers*

S. No.	*Name of the Block*	*Number of Teachers*
1.	Banki	08
2.	Badamba	09
3.	Baranga	09
4.	Cuttack Sadar	10
5.	Dampada	03
6.	Kantapada	07
7.	Mahanga	11
8.	Narsinghpur	10
9.	Niali	12
10.	Nischintakoili	10
11.	Salipur	10
12.	Cuttack Municipality	19
13.	Tangi	10
14.	Tigiria	07
15.	Choudwar MPL	05
16.	Athagarh	10
	Total	150

who was teaching life science (SCL) from each school was selected for the study. Hence, 150 secondary school science (SCL) teachers were selected as sample of the study.

From the Table 3.3 it is seen that 150 secondary school biology science teachers from Cuttack district were selected as sample of the study. The sample distribution of Cuttack district was block wise. The above table speaks that 08 teachers from Banki, 09 teachers were from Badamba, 09 teachers were from Baranga, 10 science teachers were from Cuttack Sadar, 03 from Dampada, 07 biological teachers from Kantapada, 11 were from Mahanga, 10 were from Narsinghpur, 12 were from Niali, 10 were from Nischintakoili, 10 were from Salipur, 19 biological teachers from Cuttack Municipality, 10 were from Tangi, 10 were from Tigiria, 05 were from Choudwar and 10 from Athagarh block. In order to select the experts, the researcher selected 10 experts from BSE, Odisha, different teacher training Institutions of Odisha and SCERT, Odisha.

Further, ten (10) experts from RNIASE, Cuttack, RIE, Bhubaneswar, Nalini Devi Women's College, Bhubaneswar, SCERT, Odisha, Board of Secondary Education Odisha and Rama Devi Women's University, were included in the study. The detail description of the sample is as follows. Further, Science experts of Board of Secondary Education, Odisha were also included as sample of the study.

Tools Used

Every scientific research process is through a certain well-designed tool. Tools are nothing but instruments that help the researcher to gather data. Every researcher needs data collection tools or techniques varying in design, complexity, administration, and interpretation. Each tool/technique is designed for a specific purpose. No premade instrument was identified to be suitable for the current investigation. Keeping the features of the sources and the research's aims in mind, it was chosen to employ a Opinionnaire.

To collect the requisite data, the following tools were used.

1. Self-made Opinionnaire for Biological Science Teachers
2. Self-made Opinionnaire for Biological Science Experts
3. Focused Group Discussion (FGD) for Biological Science Teachers.

Opinionnaire for Biological Science Teachers

In order to get the opinion of secondary school science teachers the researchers used the opinionnaire having three-point rating scale A (Agree), UD (Undecided), and D (Disagree), and divided into several parts according to characteristics of textbook. After reviewing related literature several types of scales were deeply studied and then suitable idea about tool creation was adopted.

The Opinionnaire consisted of seven domains which are given below.

- Physical aspects of textbook
- Printing quality of textbook
- Presentation of content
- Organization of content
- Figures, graphs and tables
- Homework, assignment and self-study material
- Reference material.

Validity of the Tool

The tool developed by the researcher was shared with 16 experts in the field of education to get their feedback on validity and functionality of the tools. The feedback were received from the experts in due course of time. The experts gave some suggestions. Changes were made as per their suggestions. Some grammatical errors and structure of the sentences were corrected as per the suggestions of the experts. The structure of the tool was also modified as per their suggestions for better clarity. Some irrelevant statements were removed as per their suggestions. The names of the experts were given in the appendix.

Content validity indices were calculated for teachers through universal agreement calculation method and found to be 0.7518 which shows the tool is valid.

Reliability of the Tool

Reliability is the second most important characteristic of a measuring device. Greene et al., 1955, say.

"Á test is said to be reliable when it functions consistently" (p.72)

In order to test the reliability of the tool, a pilot study was conducted. After the preparation of final draft of the Opinionnaire for the teachers at secondary schools of Cuttack district, the author first administered the Opinionnaire to a sample of 20 secondary schools' teachers of Cuttack municipality area. After getting their responses these are tabulated. So, to estimate the reliability of the Opinionnaire. The exercise was repeated after one month by administering the previous Opinionnaire to the same sample of teachers. Now the investigator got two sets of scores. These two sets of scores were correlated the byproduct movement method and used the statistical formula to calculate the co-efficient of correlation given by Garrett. (1971).

$$\frac{r_{xy} = \dfrac{\sum x^1 y^1}{N} - C^1 x C^1 y}{x^1 y^1}$$

Where x', y' are the deviations from the assumed mean. N is the size of the sample, c'_x, c'_y are correlation factors. The value of r found for teachers was 0.748, which is very high. Thus, the opinionnaire was highly reliable. The final version of the opinionnaire consisted of 66 items out of which six items were from Physical characteristics of textbook; Printing quality of textbook (8); Representation of content (13); Organization of content (11); Figures, graphs and tables (5); Homework, assignment and self-study material (10); and reference material (9).

Opinionnaire for Biological Science Experts

The initial draft of the Opinionnaire for experts for the evaluation of Class IX Biological Science Textbook consisted of 08 open-ended questions. After consulting many experts on different days and acting upon their expert advice and feedback, the initial draft of the Opinionnaire was modified and redrafted. The final draft of the open-ended Opinionnaire consisted of 10 questions. These 10 questions were based on different aspects of the book such as

Table 3.4 *Domain wise Distribution of Opinionnaire*

S. No.	*Domain*	*Items Teachers Opinionnaire*
1	Physical aspects of textbook	6
2	Printing quality of textbook	8
3	Presentation of content	13
4	Organization of content	11
5	Figures, graphs and tables	5
6	Homework, assignment and self-study	10
7	Reference material	9
	Total	62

Physical features, Suitability for learners, Teaching-learning content, Exercises, Language, Non-Textual Content, Syllabus and others. Out of these 10 questions, none was negative.

Focus Group Discussion (FGD) for Biological Science Teachers

A focus group discussion is a form of group interviewing in which a small group – usually 10 to 12 people – is led by a moderator (interviewer) in a loosely structured discussion of various topics of interest. The course of the discussion is usually planned in advance and most moderators rely on an outline, or moderator's guide, to ensure that all topics of interest are covered (Mishra. L 2016). A Focus Group Discussion (FGD) is a qualitative research method and data collection technique in which a selected group of people discuss a given topic or issue in-depth, facilitated by a professional, external moderator. This method serves to solicit participants' attitudes and perceptions, knowledge and experiences and practices, shared in the course of interaction with different people. Here the researcher conducted FGD for biological science teachers in different blocks of Cuttack district. Three FGDs were held, out of which one in Cuttack municipality, one in Athagarh NAC and One in Choudwar NAC. In the FGD of this study only those secondary school science teachers who are teaching Biology at Class IX participated. The researcher acted as a moderator. In FGD-1, 12 teachers participated, FGD-2, seven teachers participated, and FGD-3, nine teachers participated. Focus Group Discussions on the above theme were held in the months of February and March 2022

Procedure for Data Collection

At the first stage, the researcher collected the route chart and other required information about each sample school from the districts and block headquarters and started her journey to reach sample schools.

After reaching the school the researcher met the headmaster of the concerned school and took the permission from him to administer the Opinionnaires to the teachers. The investigator met the teacher respondents in the common room and established rapport with them. Then the researcher distributed the Opinionnaire to the teacher for collection of data. The investigator also explained how to answer the questions. The researcher tried her best to clarify all the doubts of the teachers regarding the Opinionnaire. Further, the researcher contacted the experts, established rapport and collected the information through the Opinionnaire meant for them.

No significant problems arose during the field work, however, a minor encumbrance was the road travel needed to reach the sites due to the general bad conditions of the roads in the state. Due to Covid-19 pandemic most of the schools were closed and opened on alternate days only from October 2020 – February 2021. In order to reveal the pros and cons of biological science textbook prescribed by BSE, Odisha, one of the techniques used for data collection and assessment was Focus Group Discussion (FGD). Through FGD the researcher discussed the results of evaluation of Opinionnaire confirming the findings and identified evidence that dissented with the evaluation results. To record the discussion during FGD, the researcher worked with two collaborators to audio-tape, to make the field note, and to memo the process. The results of the recorded discussion were transcribed verbatim, and the results of the field notes and memos were confirmed. This way, the method triangulation collected data from various sources and techniques was followed.

Analysis of Data

The data were analyzed both qualitatively and quantitatively. For quantitative analysis, descriptive statistics like frequency and percentage, mean and standard deviation were used. Further, t-test was used for the purpose of comparison between different groups of teachers.

Conclusion

The design of the study, procedure, population, sample, tools, reliability, validity of the tools, scoring and statistical techniques are discussed in this chapter. The collected data were analyzed by using percentage analysis followed by qualitative analysis presented in the next chapter.

IV

'Jiba Bigyan' Biological Science Textbook of Class IX

Analysis and Interpretation

> Analysis of data implies concentrating the arranged material so as to decide the inalienable certainties or implications. It includes getting ready down existing complex components into basic parts and assembling the parts in new game plan process which goes into research in one structure or the other in assurance of strategy and in translating and reaching determinations from data accumulated.
>
> – S.P. Shukla

In the words of C.V. Good, "Process of interpretation is essentially one of stating what results findings show, what do they mean? What is their significance? What is the answer to the original problem?"

Analysis means classifying, controlling and outlining the crude scores to acquire answers to research questions. The reason for the analysis is to decrease data to coherent and interpretable structure with the goal that the connection of the examination issue can be contemplated and tried.

The present section manages the analysis and translation of data. The data for the examination was gathered by soliciting the opinion of teachers and experts regarding the textbook analysis. Reactions obtained from the subject were scored following the standard scoring strategies portrayed in the separate manuals. The scores were arranged, classified and examined and the subtleties are given in the chapter. The analysis of the data was completed with the assistance of fitting measurable methods, and the findings were likewise deciphered keeping in view the objectives of the investigation and the findings were genuinely interpreted.

The Context: Biological Science Textbook of Class IX – An Introduction

The Biology (Science Part-II) textbook for Class IX is JIBA BIGYAN. The book has been authorized as per the syllabus of the Board of Secondary Education, Odisha. It has been written by Prof. Dr Tarinicharan Kar,

Prof. Pradeep Kumar Mohapatra, Dr Bijaya Kumar Mohanty. Dr Kishor Chandra Mohanty, Mr Durga Prasad Das and Dr Rajkishore Panda. The year of publication was 2016 and printed at Surekha Prints and Laxmi Web Prints, Cuttack.

Analysis stands for the process of breaking or separating a thing into its constituent smaller parts. The textbook of Biology of Class IX consists of the following chapters.

Chapter I: Biodiversity, Chapter II: Cell and its Organization, Chapter III: Tissue System, Chapter IV: Improvement of Food Resources, Chapter V: Diseases and their Treatment, and Chapter VI is Natural Resources and its Pollution.

Chapter I: The name of this chapter is 'Biodiversity'. It comprises of introduction, basic issues of scientific naming, International Code of Biological Nomenclature (ICBN), basis of classifications, hierarchy of classifications, five kingdom classifications as Monera, Protista, Fungi, Plantae and Animalia, classifications of plantae, animalia, classification of animalia like non-chordate, protochordate, vertebrata, non-vertebrata. Plants are divided into five groups such as Thallophytes, Bryophytes, Pteridophytes, Gymnosperm and Angiosperms. Animals are divided into ten groups: Porifera, Coelenterate, Platyhelminthes, Nematodes, Annelida, Arthropoda, Mollusca, Echinodermata, Protochordate and Vertebrata. There is a chart on classification of animalia. Before the end of the chapter what you have learnt and works for you is mentioned in the textbook. At the end exercises are also given in the biological science textbook.

The name of the chapter of this biological science is biodiversity. The introduction of this chapter is not very satisfactory. The life span of a few numbers of organisms is provided whereas a greater number of organisms better should be provided. In biodiversity, eco-system must be described which is not done. The pictures given in this chapter are small in size, not colourful, blurred and labelling is not very clear and attractive for the students. This chapter is lengthy, should be sub-divided into two parts. The scientific names of all the phylum and scientific terms are difficult to learn by the students. The chart of animal kingdom is provided in portrait mode, if it is provided in landscape mode it will be easily understood. Conceptual clarity is not very clear. It does not follow Bloom's taxonomy. The classification of plants and animals is not quite easily understood by children. The lessons should better be arranged from easy to difficult or simple to complex order. No lively examples given to explain the concept clearly. All the definitions and scientific terms are mentioned in English with bracket, but a few words are explained. This is a hard topic which must be given more importance. Less number of activities is given for the experiments at the end of each chapter. In this section all the important points that we learnt are not given. In the question section, descriptive questions are given more importance whereas objective questions are fewer in numbers. At the end of each chapter, reference should be given but in this chapter no reference is given.

Chapter II: The name of this chapter is "Cell and its Organization". It comprises a good introduction of cell, defining it as the structural and functional unit of life. What are living organisms made up of? What is a cell made up of and the structural organization of a cell. In this chapter the structure of cell is described, which is encircled by cell membrane inside it there is cytoplasm and nucleus are present. The cell organelles are like cell wall, mitochondria, vacuoles, endoplasmic reticulum, Golgi bodies, ribosomes, lysosomes, plastids, chromosomes and nucleus. The difference between prokaryotic cell and eucaryotic cell, plant and animal cell is discussed. Most plant cells contain plastids called as chromoplasts and leucoplasts. Chromoplasts contain chlorophyl pigment called chloroplasts which performs photosynthesis. In plant cells there is cell wall but in animal cell it is not found and at the end the complete overview of chapter is provided. In the last part, some activities there are discussed and then questions are designed.

The Introduction and Summary are not discussed elaborately. The figures of plant and animal cell are of appropriate size but are blurred and cannot be distinguished properly as per labelling. All the scientific terms are spelt in English and written in Odia. The term plastid in the page number 27 which is not explained in detail, so it does not help in clearing the concept to students. In the sub-heading nucleus, the central part of cell is nucleus which is not provided. The picture of D.N.A is given which is blurred and colourless and if it is multicolored it will capture the student's attention. In the heading of chromosome, no picture is provided which can be designed by a nice coloured picture. There are no lively examples which will clarify the student's concept. In page number 30 there are four activities given for the students, but these activities are not interesting enough to draw the attention of students. In page number 30, 2.2 there is an example of Rhoeo discolour leave for the experiment, but it is not found locally. This chapter mostly explains all the cell organelles, but the materials given cannot clear the concept fully. Few questions are given in multiple sections. There are 4 to 5 questions designed for long types. More questions should be asked. There are no questions of yes/no and true/ false. In what we learnt in this section only ten points are focused. All the important points can be included here.

Chapter III: The third chapter is "Tissue System". It describes briefly the introductory part stating it as a group of similar cells in structure and performing a single function. In this topic plant tissues are classified into two main types – meristematic and permanent. On the basis of position, it is divided into three types: apical meristem, lateral meristem and intercalary meristem. On the basis of size, position and growth, meristem is divided into two types — primary and secondary meristem. In this topic permanent tissue is classified into simple and complex tissue. Simple tissue is classified into parenchyma, collenchyma and sclerenchyma. Complex tissue is divided into xylem and phloem, xylem is comprised of four types, such as tracheid, vessel, xylem parenchyma, and xylem fiber, whereas phloem is classified into four types, such as sieve tube, companion cell, phloem parenchyma, phloem fiber. Then animal tissue is described and classified by four categories, such as epithelial tissue, connective tissue, muscle tissue, nervous tissue. There is a chart describing types of tissue is given: depending on shape and function epithelial tissue is categorized as squamous, cuboidal, columnar, ciliated and glandular. Different types of connective tissues in our body including polar tissue, adipose tissue, bone, tendon, ligament, cartilages and blood are described vividly. Different types of muscle tissues like striated, untreated and cardiac are discussed. Nervous tissue is made of neurons receiving and conducting impulses in our body. Some activities are given in this chapter. The figures of parenchyma, collenchyma, sclerenchyma, and figures of complex tissues are designed, but the figures are small in size, colourful figures and labelling of figures is not done. Appropriate and interesting activities and experiments are not given for practical purposes. In the last part objective and subjective questions are given.

In this chapter, Introduction is not appropriate to come to the main point. The sub-heading 3.1 tissue system is not discussed properly clarifying all that cell-tissue-tissue system-organ-organ system-animal/plant. This chart is necessary, but it is lacking in the textbook. In the sub-heading plant tissue and its classification, a chart is provided at the end, but it should be inserted at first instance for the easier explanation of plant tissue. Classification of plant tissue is not explained minutely so the students get confused, and they are facing problems in this chapter. All the figures of plant tissues are blurred and colourless which are not attractive, the size of picture is small, and the labelling parts are also not clear to understand. The chart of epithelial tissue is given. There must be a chart for explaining the animal tissue. Enough activities are given for the experiment but should be arranged in each part of the chapter rather than given at the end of the chapter. In 'what we learn' section, there are some important points discussed. In the question section multiple and long questions are given but true/false questions are not given. Learning outcomes and objectives are not fulfilled properly. Reference is not given at the end of the chapter.

Chapter IV: In this chapter – 'Improvement of Food Resources' – introduction about food resources is described briefly: crop yields and their improvements are given much importance. In this chapter crop variety improvements, sources of nutrient supply, manures and fertilizer which are the main sources of nutrients supply to crop, are focused. Detailed description of fertilizer and manure are discussed: It lays emphasis on organic farming, tissue culture, mixed farming, inter cropping and crop rotation. Disease control of plant varietal improvement is required for higher yield, good quality, shortening the maturity duration and wider adoptability issues are discussed. Animal husbandry mainly focusses on farm animal's proper care and management like breeding, shelter, feeding and disease control is stressed more in this chapter. A diary on account of animal husbandry is described, though the figures of various cows are given but it is blurred and not colourful so it does not arouse interest of students. For enrichment poultry farming is done to increase the production of domestic fowls, it includes both egg and broiler for poultry meat. For the better production of egg and poultry meat cross breading is done between Indian and exotic breeds for hybrid fowl. Pisciculture is described briefly, how it enhances production of fish, and they can be cultured in both marine and inland eco system of aquaculture is also discussed. Marine fish are captured by fishing net which is guided by latest technology like echo-sounder and satellite. Nowadays for enhancement of pisciculture, composite fish culture system is given highest importance. A brief discussion on bee-keeping which is used to get honey and wax is done. The activities for the students given in the book do not arouse interest in the minds of the students. A summary is described briefly and in the last part various types of questions are given as per the mental level of the students. Before the end the summary is discussed in detail. The chapter is too large, and can be divided in two units, so that the students can easily cover it.

The introduction in this chapter is not clarified properly. There is a chart which explains the disease of plants, insect pest and disease control, but only about a few crops are described in detail. In page number 59 there are various figures of cows shown but the pictures are blurred. In 4.6 poultry is discussed in detail but the pictures of different types of poultry are given in small size, and all the pictures are blurred. The pisciculture and aquaculture are described but very briefly. Activities are given at the end of the chapter. Multiple choice and descriptive questions are provided. The number of questions is appropriate to test the knowledge of the students.

Chapter V: This chapter comprises of 'Diseases and their Treatment'; the introductory part discusses health and how we can maintain good health. The significance of health is focused, both personal and community health are described and distinction between healthy and disease-free life is out lined. Focus is on diseases and their causes. What do you mean by acute and chronic disease and what is the cause of infectious and not-infectious diseases?. What are the agents and means of their spread? What prevention measures are taken for infectious diseases? Principles of prevention of diseases for healthy life are better than their successful treatment. Communicable diseases can be prevented by using immunization through vaccine or any other means. It is discussed that effective prevention of contagious diseases in the community regards that everyone should have access to public hygiene and immunization is the last part of this topic. There are few communicable diseases like typhoid, diarrhea, malaria, hepatitis, rabies, aids, tuberculosis and polio have been covered with reference to their cause symptoms, treatment and how to eradicate these diseases are discussed in this chapter. In this chapter only seven pictures are provided which are small in size, blurred and pictures are in black and white. Before the end of the chapter, what is learnt by the students is given. There should be a few objective questions arranged covering each part of the sub-topics.

In this chapter, personal and community health issues are not discussed elaborately but briefly. Distinction between healthy and disease-free person is discussed with a chart but it is discussed in paragraphs. Communicable and non-communicable diseases are given but only communicable diseases are given importance. Sufficient questions are given but more multiple-choice questions should have been be provided. A few activities are given for the experiment. In 'what we learnt' portion the important points are discussed briefly. No references are given at the end of this chapter.

Chapter VI: The name of this topic is 'Natural Resources and Its Pollution'. Introduction gives description of natural resources. The classification of natural resources, renewable resources and non-renewable resources is defined in this chapter. Life on the earth depends on resources like air, soil, water and energy from the sun. The air, role of atmosphere, the movement of the air, transpiration, rain, water, soil and its types are described in this chapter. The pollution of air, water and soil is focused. Detailed description of greenhouse effect is discussed in this chapter. How depletion of ozone layer occurs and all the biogeochemical cycles such as water cycle, oxygen cycle, carbon cycle and nitrogen cycle with detailed descriptions of charts are described but the students get confused to study so many cycles at one time. No useful activities or experiments are provided for the purpose of practical. In this chapter a number of projects are provided for the practical knowledge of students. What is learnt from the chapter is minutely discussed. Lastly, various types of questions are set for testing the knowledge of students.

In this last chapter, there should be a chart provided on the point 6.1.1 classification of natural resources. Air is discussed in 6.2 but it is very brief, components of air are tabulated. There should be short questions provided in each sub-heading. Atmosphere and the layers of atmosphere are discussed. For the explanation of atmosphere there should an appropriate graph provided. The picture which is given is attractive and easy to understand for the students. All the layers of soil are shown in the picture but in black and white which is not attractive for students. The types of pollutions of air, water and soil are discussed but not elaborately. For the explanation of the greenhouse effect there must be a good picture and the materials given are not clear to understand. The ozone layer is given but the depletion of ozone layer is not discussed clearly. There are a number of biogeochemical cycles like water cycle, oxygen cycle, carbon cycle, nitrogen cycle and water cycle provided. Nitrogen cycle and water cycle are discussed clearly but all other cycles are little bit confusing and not explained properly. The concept is not cleared. Excess numbers of activities are there, but it is not easy to execute the experiments. There are six numbers of projects provided but the materials used in this project are not found easily. In the portion what we learnt, only a few points are focused. Questions are arranged appropriately to test the knowledge of students.

From the above analysis it is revealed that the content did not address creativity and innovation skill. Few topics from all the chapters encouraged the very initial form of critical thinking among students with no questions or activities asking for the use of problem-solving ability. No lively examples given to explain the concept clearly. All the definitions and scientific terms are mentioned in English with bracket, but a few words are explained. Majority of the content of the book followed an organized structure and sequence. The explanation of the concepts had a sequence of description of concept, example, uses and disadvantages. The language and words used were apprehensible. However, most of the pictures and diagrams used were not of high quality and clear. A well-organized written explanation can promote the ability to explain something clearly. But the variety of skills needed for verbal and nonverbal communication were not urged as any group activity or classroom activity for collaborative work was not suggested in the chapters. Moreover, opportunities to work with teams to accomplish a goal were not proposed in the content. No topic in the book advocated the development of information literacy skill. Even the questions provided in the exercise can be answered just by looking at the information provided in the chapters. In two chapters, number of questions is more in the exercises. Information and literacy skills are demanded from students in the contemporary world to search and evaluate material from multiple sources to resolve a problem. But the development of media literacy, Information and Communication Technology (ICT) literacy, productivity and accountability, leadership and responsibility skills were not promoted through any of the content of the book. Only one topic addressed the promotion of skill of flexibility and adaptability. The advancement of social and cross-cultural skills was observed to be addressed by only one topic containing basic information about how an animal society is formed. There was no activity/ project found in the chapters to encourage the development/

exercise of the soft skills. As far as the interdisciplinary skills are concerned, four topics addressed the need of students of global awareness. A number of topics promoted health literacy among students. However, it was noticed that the chapters were too much focused on the provision of large amount of information rather than developing and making use of information processing skill of students. The above analysis said that the biological science textbook of Class IX followed the objectives of Board of Secondary Education, Odisha. The textbook did not address the different components of NCF 2005 i.e., the development of flexibility and adaptability, creativity and innovation, and leadership and responsibility skills.

Opinion of Biological Science Teachers on Content of Textbook

Objective No. 1: To examine the opinion of secondary school biological science teachers on content of Biological Science Textbook of Class IX as per the objective prescribed by Board of Secondary Education, Odisha

General Profile of Teachers

From the Table 4.1 it is found that 24 per cent of science teachers are male and 76 per cent are female. With regard to educational qualification 63 per cent secondary school science teachers of Odisha teaching SCL are B.Sc. B.Ed., 08 per cent are B.Sc. M.Ed., 21 per cent are M.Sc. B.Ed., 04 per cent are M.Phil. and 01 per cent are having Ph.D. qualification. Similarly, with respect to experience 45 per cent of the respondents are having above 10 years of teaching experience and 55 per cent of the respondents are having less than 10 years of teaching experience.

Table 4.1: *General Profile of Teachers*

S. No.	*Profile*		*%*
1	Gender	Male	24
		Female	76
2	Educational Qualification	B.Sc. B.Ed.	63
		B.Sc M.Ed.	08
		M.Sc. B.Ed.	21
		M.Sc. M.Ed.	03
		M.Phil., M.Ed.	04
		Ph.D.	01
3	Experience	Above 10 years	45
		Below 10 Years	55

Opinion of Secondary School Biological Science Teachers on the Content of Biological Science Textbook of Class IX as per the Objective Prescribed by Board of Secondary Education, Odisha

The biological science textbook has been prepared as per the National Curriculum Framework-2005 and State Curriculum Framework-2007. The book contains preamble of the Constitution in order to inculcate moral values among the students. The content of the book has been arranged in order to develop scientific aptitude and to acquire various scientific skills which would be essential for 21st century skills. Thus, opinion has been sought from biology teachers and has been presented in the Table 4.2.

From the Table 4.2 it is seen that 70 per cent of biological science teachers agreed that the selection of the content of the textbook was as per the guiding principles of NCF-2005 and SCF-2007. Whereas 80 per cent of the respondents agreed that selection of content was appropriate for developing scientific aptitude among the learners. Sixty five percent (65 per cent) of teachers agreed that the topic and sub-topic of biological science textbook are appropriate for developing scientific inquiry and creativity. Similarly, 87 per cent of teachers agreed that the content will be helpful in developing questioning skill for acquiring further knowledge among the learners. Only 43 per cent of teachers agreed that the textbook will be helpful for students to acquire different skills required for 21st

Table 4.2: *Opinion of Secondary School Biological Science Teachers on the Content of Biological Science Textbook as per BSE, Odisha*

S. No.	*Statements*	*Agree* %	*Disagree* %	*Undecided* %
1	Content is arranged as per the principles of NCF 2005 and SCF 2007	70	23	07
2	Selection of content is appropriate for developing scientific aptitude	80	13	7
3	The topic and sub-topic are appropriate for developing scientific inquiry and creativity	65	20	15
4	The content will be helpful in developing questioning skill for acquiring further knowledge	87	09	04
5	The textbook will be helpful for students to acquire different skills required for 21st century skills	43	39	18

century skills, whereas 39 per cent of teachers disagree to the above statement and 18 per cent of teachers undecided for the same.

Opinion of Teachers on Different aspects of Biological Science Textbook of Class IX

Objective No. 2: To assess the opinion of secondary school biological science teachers on following aspects of Biological Science Textbook of Class IX such as:

- *Cover and back page*
- *Printing quality*
- *Get-up*
- *Binding*
- *Cost and availability*
- *Selection of topic and sub-topic*
- *Presentation of content*
- *Organization of content*
- *Languages used*
- *Diagrams, facts and figures*
- *Illustrations and examples*
- *Evaluations and exercises.*

Objective No. 3: To compare the opinions of secondary school biological science teachers on physical and academic aspects of Biological Science Textbook of Class IX having teaching experience below 10 years and above 10 years.

The objective of the study to assess the opinion of secondary school biological science teachers on various aspects of Biological Science Textbook of Class IX. The textbook has been prepared by experienced teachers and experts and lessons have been transacted by the biological science teachers at secondary schools of Odisha. Teachers are practitioner of textbook. Their perceptions are important with respect to their experience (below 10 years and above 10 years). Their perceptions have been collected through a self-made opinionnaire and tabulated in the following tables.

Opinion of Teachers on Physical Aspects of Biological Science Textbook

Physical aspects can be defined as those elements visible to the eye, specifically the physical elements. This simply means the first thing you see when you look at someone or something. Structures can be defined as the arrangement of and relations between the parts or elements of something complex. It can also be defined as the way that something is built, arranged or organized. The physical aspects of the prescribed textbooks were analyzed in terms of the textbook cover design, printing and layout, font size, prices, quality of paper. The opinion of teachers on physical aspects of Biological Science Textbook is given in the Table 4.3.

Table 4.3: *Opinion of Teachers on Physical Aspects of Biological Science Textbook of Class IX*

		Agree	*Disagree*	*Undecided*
S. No.	*Statements*	*%*	*%*	*%*
1	Cover page is attractive	58	35	07
2	Size of textbook is appropriate	37	54	9
3	Binding is not compact	68	14	18
4	Price is affordable	88	09	03
5	Quality of paper is not good	85	5	10
6	Cover page is according to subject	79	18	03

The above table speaks about the physical aspect of biological science Textbook of Class IX. From the Table 4.3 it is seen that 58 per cent of science teachers agreed that cover page of the biological science textbook is attractive, 35 per cent disagree with the statement and 07 per cent are undecided. With regard to size of textbook whether it is appropriate 37 per cent of respondents agreed, 54 per cent disagreed and 9 per cent are undecided. The binding of the biological science textbook of Class IX is not compact agreed by 68 per cent of science teachers and disagreed by 14 per cent science teachers. The price of the book is affordable, agreed by 88 per cent respondents and 09 per cent respondents disagreed. Similarly, with respect to quality of the textbook 85 per cent of science teachers agreed that quality of the paper is not good and cover page is according to the subject responded by 79 per cent of science teachers.

Table 4.4: *Teaching Experience-wise Comparison of Teachers' Opinions about Physical Aspects of Science Textbook of Class IX*

Teaching Experience	*N*	*Mean*	*SD*	*t-Value*	*p-value*
Below 10 years	68	133.68	12.05	-1.063	.273
Above 10 years	82	142.13	19.27		

The above-mentioned Table shows that the acquired p-value for under ten years or even more than ten years teaching experience secondary school science teachers of Odisha is actually (p>.05) larger compared to the .05 degree of significance. Hence, there's no big difference between the teachers' opinions about physical aspects of biological science textbook of Class IX of BSE Odisha of under ten years teaching experience (M = 133.68, SD = 12.05) or even more ten years teaching experience (M = 142.13, SD = 19.27) secondary school science teachers of Odisha at .05 level of significance, 't (148) = - 1.063, p =.273. Hence the hypothesis is rejected with respect to Physical aspect of Class IX textbook.

- ✓ Cover page is not attractive
- ✓ Quality of the paper is not good
- ✓ Binding is not durable
- ✓ Price is reasonable

In the FGD-1 it is revealed that the cover page of the textbook is not attractive, paper quality is bad. One teacher said the quality of the paper is not good by the price of the textbook. It should be improved. In all the FGDs it is found that the binding is not durable. It should be made durable even if it raises its price. The price of the book is Rs. 30.00, which is quite reasonable and within the reach of students coming from lower strata of society. No doubt the price of the book depends upon the paper used, printing, designing, illustrations and binding. It would be worthwhile to enhance its price for the improvement of the textbook. The reason being that the physical aspects of the Biological Science Textbook is weak and the pictures on the cover page are not attractive. The pictures are also not colourful and attractive. Moreover, caption of the pictures is missing, thus the pictures are carrying little importance.

Opinion of Teachers on Printing Quality

Textbooks must have good binding that makes them easy to open. Good quality binding also ensures that the book lasts for a longer period. Loosely bound textbooks will discourage the students from studying them.

The Table 4.5 talks about the printing quality of biological science book of Class IX. From the above Table it is observed that 58 per cent of science teachers agreed that the printing is not attractive, 35 per cent disagreed with this statement and 07 per cent are undecided. With regard to printing is clean 67 per cent science teachers agreed, 20 per cent disagreed with this statement and 13 per cent are undecided.

Table 4.5: *Opinion of Teachers about Printing Quality*

S. No.	*Statement*	*Agree Percentage*	*Disagree Percentage*	*Undecided Percentage*
1	Printing is not attractive.	58	35	07
2	Printing is clean and Clear	67	20	13
4	Letters are not of proper size.	74	20	06
5	Small and big letters are used appropriately	16	79	05
6	Proper page margin is given	75	21	04
7	Printing in two column made easiness in reading	66	26	08
8	Use of more than one colour make printing effective	87	07	06

With regard to the statement letters are not in proper size is agreed by 74 per cent, disagreed by 20 per cent and undecided by 06 per cent of SCL teachers. Small and big letters are used appropriately is agreed by 16 per cent, disagreed by 79 per cent and undecided by 05 per cent. Similarly with respect to proper page margin is provided is agreed by 75 per cent, disagreed by 21 per cent and undecided by 04 per cent of the respondents. The statement printing in two columns made easiness in reading is agreed by 66 per cent, disagreed by 26 per cent and undecided by 8 per cent of the biological science teachers. With regard to the use of more than one colour making printing effective is agreed by 87 per cent, disagreed by 7 per cent and undecided by 6 per cent was the response of science teachers.

Table 4.6: *Teaching Experience-wise Comparison of Teachers' Opinions about Printing Quality of Biological Science Textbook*

Teaching Experience	*Mean*	*SD*	*t-Value*	*p-value*
Below 10 years	134.75	13.05	-1.003	.265
Above 10 years	152.23	14.27		

The above-mentioned Table shows that the acquired p-value for under ten years or even more than ten years teaching experience secondary school science teachers of Odisha is actually ($p>.05$) is larger compared to the .05 degree of significance. Hence, there's no big difference between the teachers' opinions about printing quality of biological science textbook of Class IX of BSE Odisha of under ten years teaching experience ($M = 134.75$, $SD = 13.05$) or even more than ten years teaching experience ($M = 152.23$, $SD = 14.27$) secondary school science teachers of Odisha at .05 level of significance, 't (148) = - 1.003, p =. 265. Hence the hypothesis -2 is rejected with respect to printing quality of Class IX biological science textbook.

In the FGD-1 most of the teachers said that in the Biological Science Textbook some key terms have been written in bold which catch the eye of the readers very easily. Thus, some other terms in the book also needed to be written in bold. Font size of the text is such that it does not strain the eyes was also said by the respondents in FGD-2. Pictures for illustrating different concepts are appropriate were coming from the FGD-3.

One teacher said that majority of the students find water mark as a hindrance in reading the different words in different chapters. The book is not entirely free from printing mistakes also come out from the focus group discussions. Paper used for the biological science textbook of Class IX is not of good quality. The paper used for the book looks roughed up or recycled paper and is not durable at all which will withstand a whole year or session. With regard to page margin one science teacher from Athagarh said that it looks like one inch page margin on each side has been maintained. The teachers' opinions about printing quality of Biological Science Textbook are weak and moreover the printing is not attractive. Though the printing is clean and clear, the letters are not in proper size, proper page margin provided is small and big letters are not used appropriately. Printing in two columns has made reading easy but use of more than one colour would make more effective and attractive but, in this book, only black colour is used.

Opinion of Teachers on Presentation of Content

Textbooks assist in managing a lesson. It saves time, gives direction to lessons, guide discussion, facilitate in giving homework, making teaching easier, better organized, more convenient.

From the Table 4.7 it is found that the presentation of content is easily understandable by 70 per cent of the respondents and 23 per cent of the respondents do not agreed with this statement. From this Table it is inferred that 50 per cent of the respondents agreed that there are some mistakes in punctuation marks and spelling, 35 per cent disagreed and 15 per cent have given undecided statement. About 66 per cent of respondents agreed that the language and wordings of content is not designed according to the age of the students, 21 per cent of the respondents disagreed and 13 per cent

Table 4.7: *Opinion of Teachers about Presentation of Content*

S. No.	*Statements*	*Agree Percentage*	*Disagree Percentage*	*Undecided Percentage*
1.	Presentation of content is easily understandable	70	23	07
2.	Mistakes in punctuation marks and spelling are seen	50	35	15
3.	Language and wording of content are not according to the age of students	66	21	13
4.	Amount of content is enough to teach during semester	30	56	14
5.	Introduction and summary are useful	59	29	12
6.	Enough examples are not given to clarify the content	22	63	05
7.	Definitions are clearly presented	69	24	07
8.	Presentation of scientific terms are not easily understandable	66	25	09
9.	Scientific terms should be mentioned also in English	58	24	18
10.	Syllabus is lengthy according to annual exam	53	34	12
11.	Presentation of terms and symbols are not uniform	57	29	14
12.	Selection of content is according to educational objectives	30	65	05
13.	Content is not presented in logical sequence.	61	26	13

are undecided on this statement. From the Table it is studied that 56 per cent of the teachers disagreed to the statement that the amount of content is enough to teach during semester, 30 per cent agreed and 12 per cent are undecided on this statement. It is seen that 59 per cent of the science teachers agreed to that the introduction and summary are useful and 29 per cent respondents disagreed and 12 per cent are undecided to the above statement. On account of the statement not enough examples are given to clarify the content, 63 per cent of respondents disagreed and 22 per cent agreed. About 69 per cent of the respondents agreed that the definitions are clearly presented in the textbook of biological science and 24 per cent are not agreeable on it. From the above table it is studied that about 66 per cent of the respondents agreed on presentation of scientific terms are not easily understandable and 25 per cent do not agree. 58 per cent of the respondents agreed that the scientific terms should be mentioned in English, out of them 24 per cent disagreed. On the basis of syllabus of textbook is lengthy according to semester 53 per cent respondents agreed and 34 per cent do not agree to this statement. About 57 per cent of the science teachers agreed that the presentation of terms and symbols are not uniform and 29 per cent of the teachers disagreed. Nearly 65 per cent of the respondents do not agree that the selection of content is according to educational objective and 30 per cent agreed to this statement. 61 per cent of the respondents agreed that the content is not presented in a logical sequence.

Table 4.8: *Teaching Experience-wise Comparison of Teachers' Opinions about Presentation of Content of Biological Science Textbook*

Teaching Experience	*N*	*Mean*	*SD*	*t-Value*	*p-value*
Below 10 years	68	134.75	13.05	-1.003	.265
Above 10 years	82	152.23	14.27		

The above-mentioned Table shows that the acquired p-value for under ten years or even more than ten years teaching experience secondary school science teachers of Odisha is actually (p>.05) larger compared to the .05 degree of significance. Hence, there's no big difference between the teachers' opinions about printing quality of biological science textbook of Class IX of BSE Odisha of under ten years teaching experience (M = 134.75, SD = 13.05) or even more than ten years teaching experience (M = 152.23, SD = 14.27) secondary school science teachers of Odisha at .05 level of significance, 't (148) = - 1.003, p =. 265. Hence the hypothesis -1 is rejected with respect to presentation of content of Class IX Biological Science Textbook.

In all the FGDs it is found that most of the teachers said the subject matter of Biology is topically or functionally presented in a logical way in the Class IX biological Science book. One teacher from Choudwar municipality having 20 years of teaching experience said that the analysis of the textbook shows that the content of the textbook is organized very logically. Contents in the book are according to mental maturity of the students. One teacher having experience of 15 years expressed that selection of content is according to educational objectives. Content has been selected appropriately as per the aims and objectives of biological science teaching. The book is based on scientific information and previous experience of the student received in the previous grades. However, some concepts in the book have been narrowly discussed.

Demonstration and Problem-solving aspect of the method of teaching is not highlighted. From all the FGDs it is found that topics have been organized as per psychological principles, i.e. easy to difficult, simple to complex, known to unknown, concrete to abstract. Similarly, teachers opined that topics have not been organized to arouse interest to study plants and animals. Results of interview during FGD reveal that all participants indicate that when developing the textbooks, the author did not consider the student's needs, so those needs assessments were not conducted. The findings dissent with the opinions of some experts (Ur, 1996; Mukundan, 2011; Sahim, 2020; Monbec, 2020; Lawrence, 2011) who claim that needs analysis is the primary requisite for teaching materials development including the textbook. Some features that indicate the shortcoming of the textbook due to the absence of the needs assessment include neither learning objectives are well-developed nor the content scopes are properly sequenced.

In FGD-2 it is revealed that learning outcomes are not mentioned in the biological science textbook. The biological science teacher's opinion about presentation of content of Biological Science Textbook does not satisfy all. There are few spelling mistakes and punctuation marks. Maximum respondents opined that the language and wordings should be according to the age of the student. Teachers viewed that the amount of content is larger for the formative examinations. Most of the respondents are giving positive response to introduction and summary saying it is useful but more examples need to be given to clarify the content. Presentations of scientific terms are not easily understandable; syllabus is lengthy as per the content. Selection of the content is not constructed as per the educational objectives and the content is not presented in logical sequence.

- ✓ ***content of the textbook is organized very logically.***
- ✓ ***Content has been selected appropriately as per the aims and objectives***
- ✓ ***topic have not been organized as to arouse interest to study plants and animals.***
- ✓ ***Students need has not been taken care of***

Opinion of Teachers on Organization of Content

Content pages are organized to be useful to a wide range of users. They provide a definition and simple overview to the topic, as well as linked references to the most important information about that topic that is available in print. They can also contain additional detail that is useful for students, or to explore questions that are a source of active debate within the profession.

Table 4.9: *Opinion of Teachers on Organization of Content*

S. No.	*Statement*	*Agree*	*Disagree*	*Undecided*
1.	Aim of textbook is suitable for mental capability of students.	46	38	16
2.	Study of content is useful to develop scientific attitude.	50	29	21
3.	Content is not co-related with daily life.	75	15	10
4.	Textbook is helpful to teacher for using effective methods of teaching.	76	17	07
5.	Principles, concepts, formulas, examples and experiments are realistic.	89	09	02
6.	Content is organized according to psychological point of view.	75	14	11
7.	Enough weightage is not given on required topics.	49	29	22
8.	Units, symbols, and formulas are not according to scientific notations.	52	34	14
9.	Activities and additional information are useful to clarify content.	78	14	08
10.	Examples are co-related with real life.	65	34	01
11.	Content is not consistent with content of Class IX.	37	52	10

From the Table 4.9 it is observed that there are 46 per cent of the respondents who agreed with the statement that aim of textbook is suitable for mental capability of students, 38 per cent of the respondents disagreed and 16 per cent are undecided. From the Table it is interpreted that there are 50 per cent of the respondents who agreed to the statement that the study of content is useful to develop scientific attitude, 29 per cent respondents disagreed and out of them 21 per cent are undecided. There are 75 per cent of the science teachers who agreed to the statement that the content is not correlated with daily life, 15 per cent disagreed and 10 per cent are undecided in their opinion. From this table it is analyzed that 76 per cent of the respondents agreed on the statement textbook is helpful to teacher for using effective methods of teaching and 17 per cent disagreed and 7 per cent are undecided on this point. From the tabulation it is studied that principles, concepts, formulas, examples and experiments are realistic, is agreed by 89 per cent of the respondents and 09 per cent of the science teachers are disagreeing to this statement. The statement content is organized according to psychological point of view; it is found from the Table that 75 per cent of the science teachers agreed and 14 per cent of the science teachers are disagreed. From the Table it is found that 49 per cent of the science teachers agreed, 29 per cent disagreed and 22 per cent are undecided on the context of enough weightage is not given on required topics. Table 4.9 said that there are 52 per cent of the science teachers agreed on units, symbols and formulas are not according to scientific notations and 34 per cent of the respondents disagreed. From the Table it is inferred that 78 per cent of the science teachers agreed, 14 per cent disagreed on the statement activities and additional information are useful to clarify the content. There are 65 per cent of the respondents who agreed and 34 per cent disagreed on the statement that the examples are co-related with real life. From the Table it is observed that 52 per cent of the respondents disagreed, 37 per cent agreed and 10 per cent are undecided on the statement that the content is not consistent with content Biological Science Textbook of Class IX.

Table 4.10: *Teaching Experience-wise Comparison of Teachers' Opinions about Organization of Content of biological science Textbook*

Secondary School Teachers	*Mean*	*SD*	*t-Value*	*p-value*
Below 10 Years Teaching Experience Teachers	163.82	17.50	-3.090	.003
Above 10 Years Teaching Experience Teachers	175.00	17.74		

The obtained p-value for mean scores of teachers' opinions about organization of content of biological science textbook of under ten years and above ten years teaching experience of science teachers is actually ($p <.05$) under the .05 level of significance. Hence, there's a tremendous distinction between the opinions about organization of content of biological science textbook of under ten years teaching experience ($M = 163.82$, $SD = 17.50$) and above ten years teaching experience ($M = 175.00$, $SD = 17.74$) science teachers of Odisha at .05 level of significances' (ninety-eight) = 3.090, p =.033. The hostile gain scores favour previously ten years teaching experience teachers. Hence the hypothesis is accepted with respect to organization of content of Class IX Biological Science Textbook. Therefore, the opinion of above ten years' science teachers found to differ when compared to the under ten years teaching experience of science co teachers with respect to about organization of content of Biological Science Textbook of Class IX.

In the FGD-1 one teacher from Cuttack municipality having 23 years of teaching experience said that the examples contained in the book are not enough to strengthen the student's understanding of the biological concept in the Class IX biological science book prescribed by BSE, Odisha. Some biological concept of the book is related to the daily life of the student. In FGD-2 it is found that the experiments and activities in the book are compatible with its biological content. The activities are not suitable for the needs of the students. One female biology teacher of secondary school of Cuttack Municipality having M.Sc. (Botany) and B.Ed. opined that scientific names of plants and animals have not been properly written in the book and difficulty level of contents in the book is moderate. Similarly, one teacher having qualification B.Sc. B.Ed. expressed that there is not a single chapter in the Biology book which is wholly and solely devoted to the state. She also said that certain pictures related to different concepts could have been taken from the local culture to make the book more comfortable and interesting for the students. From all the FGDs it is found that no ambiguity is seen in presentation of subject matter and the diagrammatic representations need improvement and should be appropriately labeled. Figures tied in textual material by direct reference also need improvement. One teacher expressed that the topics are equally distributed, and the units are long enough and comprehensive. The biological science book should incorporate both individual and group work. Each chapter starts with a brief introduction with all key concepts. One teacher having M.Sc. M.Ed. expressed that the level of activities is not arranged as per Bloom's taxonomy. The activities, experiments suggested in the textbook are not suitable to follow constructivist approach of teaching. Similarly, Information and Communication Technology (ICT) components are missing in biological science textbook of Class IX prescribed BSE, Odisha. One teacher said detailed discussion has not been done properly in each chapter and the book helps in development of skill of conducting experiment and drawing the pictures and charts. Many teachers expressed that book provides knowledge about the habit, adaptation and life process of different plants and animals and different systems, processes in the human body. The book is helpful in developing thinking, reasoning and creative power among the students.

From the complete interpretation of the table, it is studied that the science teacher's opinion about the organization of the content is useful. Majority of the science teachers agreed the aim of textbook is suitable for mental capability of students. Most of the respondents are satisfied that the content is useful for scientific attitude but the science teachers are not satisfied with the content as it is not co-related with daily life.

- ✓ ***Examples are not enough.***
- ✓ ***scientific name of plants and animals have not been properly written in the book***
- ✓ ***Chapters are not written with respect to local context***
- ✓ ***Diagrams need improvement***
- ✓ ***Individual and group work need to be incorporated.***

From the above discussion it is found that more the science teachers are satisfied on principles, concepts, formulas, examples and experiments are realistic, content of the textbook is organized, activities and additional information are useful to clarify the content, examples given in the textbook are co-related with real life. From above discussions it is observed that most of the respondents are dissatisfied that enough weightage has not been given to the required topic, units, symbols and formulas are not designed according to scientific notations, content is not co-related with daily life and the content is not consistent with content of standard IX.

Opinion of Teachers on Figures, Graphs and Tables

Visual elements such as graphs, charts, tables, photographs, diagrams, and maps capture students' attention and help them to understand the scientific ideas more fully.

Table 4.11: *Opinion of Teachers on Figures, Graphs and Tables*

Sr.	*Statement*	*Agree*	*Disagree*	*Undecided*
1	Enough figures are given in textbook	74	21	05
2	Pictures and figures are not of proper size	100	00	00
3	Enough figures with nomenclature are given to clarify content	100	00	00
4	Enough figures and tables are given in experiments	25	75	00
5	Figures are given on proper places.	95	00	05

(The figure in the numerator indicates the number and that of the denominators indicate the corresponding percentage)

From the above table it is inferred that 74 per cent of the respondents agreed to the statement enough figures are given in textbook, 21 per cent of the respondents disagreed on it. All the 100 per cent respondents agreed on the statement pictures and figures are not of proper size. From the table it is observed that all the 100 per cent respondents agreed on enough figures with nomenclature are given to clarify content. Most of the science teachers, about 75 per cent are disagreed with the statement enough figures and tables are given in experiment and 25 per cent of the respondents agreed to this statement. Most of the science teachers, about 95 per cent are satisfied that the figures are given at proper places and 5 per cent are undecided.

Table 4.12: *Teaching Experience-wise Comparison of Teachers' Opinions about Figures, Graphs and Tables of Biological Science Textbook*

Secondary School Teachers	*Mean*	*SD*	*t-Value*	*p-value*
Below 10 Years Teaching Experience Teachers	154.75	18.50	-3.189	.007
Above 10 Years Teaching Experience Teachers	178.00	18.74		

The obtained p-value for mean scores of teachers' opinions about figures, graphs and tables Biological Science Textbook of under ten years and above ten years teaching experience of science teachers is actually (p <.05) under the .05 level of significance. Hence, there's a tremendous distinction between the opinions about organization of content of biological science textbook of under ten years teaching experience and above ten years teaching experience of science teachers of Odisha at .05 level of significance, 't (ninety-eight) = 3.189, p =.007. The hostile gain scores favour previously ten years teaching experience teachers. Hence the hypothesis is accepted with respect to opinions about figures, graphs and tables of Class IX biological science textbook. Therefore, the opinion of above ten years' science teachers was found to differ compared to the less than ten years teaching experience of science teachers with respect to figures, graphs and tables of Biological Science Textbook of Class IX.

In all the FGDs it was found that enough figures are given in textbook and pictures and figures are not of proper size. The labeling of the picture is not good. Negligible pictures are blured which do not clear the concept of the students. Thus, it is clear from the above analysis that quality and quantity of figures, tables and charts are satisfactory.

From the complete discussion of the table, it is found that most of the science teachers are satisfied on the statements enough figures are given in the textbook, maximum figures with nomenclature are given to clarify content and figures are given at proper places of the textbook. It is also observed that most of the respondents are not satisfied with the proper size of pictures and figures and enough figures and tables are not disagreeing with the experiments. Hence from the analysis of the table it is observed that quality and quantity of figures, tables and charts are appreciated.

Opinion of Teachers on Homework, Assignment and Self-study Materials

Homework allows students to revise classroom learnings and builds the habit of self-study. This helps them to score better. While doing homework, students concentrate on the textbook.

Table 4.13: *Opinion of Teachers on Homework, Assignment and Self-study Materials*

S. No.	*Statement*	*Agree*	*Disagree*	*Undecided*
1.	Questions for self-study are given at the end of every chapter	74	21	05
2.	All topics have been provided with evaluation questions/ exercises.	100	00	00
3.	Enough objective type questions are not given	100	00	00
4.	Every type of question is given in exercises	25	75	00
5.	Answers of every question can be found within content	95	00	05
6.	Self-study questions are useful to strengthen content	58	35	07
7.	Format of questions are not proper	02	88	10
8.	Exercises are useful to enhance self-study	100	00	00
9.	Questions are not repeated elsewhere.	94	04	02
10.	Questions are framed properly and free from ambiguity.	95	00	05

Table 4.13 reveals Teachers' Opinions about Homework, Assignment and Self Study Materials. Questions and home assignments play a critical role in the book for the students and teachers. In the Biological Science Textbook Questions for self-study are given at the end of every chapter opined by 74 per cent of secondary teachers. Almost all teachers (150 in number) said that all

topics have been provided with evaluation questions/ exercises and enough objective type questions are not given. With regard to every type of questions is given in exercises 75 per cent teachers disagree with the statement. Ninety-Five (95 per cent) percentage of teachers said that answers to every question can be found within content and 58 per cent respondents opined that self-study questions are useful to strengthen content. With respect to the statement format of questions are not proper 88 per cent teachers disagreed. Almost all the teachers agreed that exercises are useful to enhance self-study. Similarly, 94 per cent of teachers said that questions are not repeated elsewhere and 95 per cent agreed that questions are framed properly and free from ambiguity.

Table 4.14: *Teaching Experience-wise Comparison of Teachers' Opinions about Homework, Assignment and Self-study Materials*

Teaching Experience	*N*	*Mean*	*SD*	*t-Value*	*p-value*
Below 10 years	68	169.93	16.06	-1.007	.267
Above 10 years	82	172.19	17.28		

The above-mentioned table shows that the acquired p-value for under ten years or even more than ten years teaching experience secondary school science teachers of Odisha is actually ($p>.05$) larger compared to the .05 degree of significance. Hence, there's no big difference between the teachers' opinions about homework, assignment and self-study materials of under ten years teaching experience (M = 169.93, SD = 16.06) or even more than ten years teaching experience (M = 172.19, SD = 17.28) secondary school science teachers of Odisha at .05 level of significance, 't (148) = - 1.107, p =. 267. Hence the hypothesis -1 is rejected with respect to homework, assignment and self-study Materials of Class IX Biological Science Textbook.

In the FGD-1 one teacher highlighted that the objective type questions are not given as per the bloom's taxonomy i.e., Knowledge, Understanding, Application and Skill. The higher order questions are not found in the biological science textbook. In the FGD-2 almost all said that the questions are not encouraging the students to acquire the knowledge, manners and behaviours that they do not have earlier. Specific skill type questions are missing in the biological science textbook. With regard to self-study material, the questions will not encourage the students to score more marks in the annual examination of Class IX revealed in FGD-3.

Similarly, most of the exercises are according to the subject matter but not the realistic environment of the students found in FGD-2. More questions on application and skill based should be included in the biological science textbook of Class IX of BSE, Odisha was opined by many teachers in FGD-1, FGD-2 and FGD-3. The exercises are not graded for slow, average and gifted learners were also revealed by the teachers in the FGD-1. One teacher of Cuttack Municipality said in the FGD that not a single chapter in the book contains URL(s) (Uniform Resource Locator) as they are helpful in gaining additional knowledge about the different concepts in the book. Moreover URL must be given in each chapter which adds a dimension to biological science book.

From the above analysis it is found that homework assignment is given at the end of each chapter of the textbook. Sufficient number of objective type questions is not given in the book. Self-study materials are not given in the book. Answers to every question are found within content; questions are not repeated elsewhere and questions are framed properly and free from any ambiguity. There is no significant difference between male and female teachers' opinion about homework, assignment and self-study materials given in the biological science textbook of Class IX prescribed by BSE Odisha. Similarly with respect to teaching experience there's no big difference between the secondary school science teachers of Odisha of under ten years teaching experience or even more than ten years teaching experience opinions about homework, assignment and self-study materials given in the biological science textbook prescribed by BSE, Odisha.

Opinion of Teachers on Reference Material

Reference materials are of critical importance in establishing comparability and accuracy of analytical results between different locations and over time.

The Table 4.15 speaks about teachers' opinions about reference material. From the above table it is seen that 94 per cent of teachers said that the book has not cited appropriate number of reference books for teachers and students and 04 per cent disagreed. With regard to alphabetical index all the teachers said that it is not given in the biological science textbook of Class IX. Similarly, all the teachers agreed that reference materials are not given after every chapter. Proper guidance for use of textbook for teacher is given was

Table 4.15: *Opinion of Teachers on Reference Material*

S. No.	*Statement*	*Agree*	*Disagree*	*Undecided*
1.	The book has not cited appropriate number of reference books for teachers and students.	94	04	02
2.	Alphabetical index is not given.	100	00	00
3.	Reference materials are not given after every chapter.	100	00	00
4.	Proper guidance for use of textbook for teacher is given.	21	79	00
5.	Exercises are lengthy.	14	84	02
6.	Deep understanding of experimental work is not given.	58	35	07
7.	Enough synonyms for scientific term should be given	84	14	02
8.	The glossary of the book is rich enough and does not require any other dictionary.	02	88	10
9.	website addresses given in all chapters.	00	100	00

agreed by 21 per cent and disagreed by 79 per cent. Fourteen (14 per cent) teachers agreed that exercise is lengthy whereas 84 per cent teachers are disagreeing with this statement. With regard to deep understanding of experimental work is not given, 58 per cent teachers agreed and 35 per cent disagreed to the above statement. Enough synonyms for scientific term should be given is agreed by 84 per cent of the teachers, the glossary of the book is rich enough and does not require any other dictionary is agreed by a very negligible percentage of teachers, i.e., 2 per cent. Similarly, all the teachers agreed that website addresses not given in all chapters.

Table 4.16: *Teaching Experience-wise Comparison of Teachers' Opinions about Reference Material*

Teaching Experience	*N*	*Mean*	*SD*	*t-Value*	*p-value*
Below 10 years	68	154.93	14.05	-1.006	.273
Above 10 years	82	163.19	16.29		

The above-mentioned table shows that the acquired p-value for under ten years or even more than ten years teaching experience secondary school science teachers of Odisha is actually (p>.05) larger compared to the .05 degree of significance. Hence, there's no big difference between the teachers' opinions about reference material of less than ten years teaching experience or even more than ten years teaching experience secondary school science teachers of Odisha at .05 level of significance. Hence the hypothesis is rejected with respect to reference materials of Class IX biological science textbook.

In the FGD-1 one teacher expressed that proper guidance for use of textbook for teachers is lacking in the biological science textbook. Similarly, one teacher having more than 10 years of teaching experience said that it will be useful if reference material is given at the end of each chapter. In FGD-2 researcher found that experimental work must be given at the end of the chapter. The glossary of the book is not given in the textbook.

From the above analysis it is found that book has not cited appropriate number of reference books for teachers and students, alphabetical index is not given, reference materials are not given after every chapter, proper guidance for use of textbook for teacher is not given, deep understanding of experimental work is not given and website addresses not given in all chapters of biological science book of Class IX prescribed by BSE, Odisha. On having a proper look at the contents in the book it was found that there are certain concepts which have been narrowly discussed thus teachers need some supplementary material for such concepts to make them understand by students.

Overall Assessment of Biological Science Textbook of Class IX

Table 4.17: *Criteria for Interpretation*

Level	*Range*	*Range of Scores*
High	Above Mean+1SD	20.7 – 25.0
Moderate	Mean – 1SD to mean + 1SD	12.1 – 20.7
Low	Below mean – 1SD	00 – 12.1

From the above Table it is revealed that the mean scores of opinions of teachers on various aspects of biological science textbook varied. The maximum and minimum possible scores were 25 and 00 (zero) respectively, the mean scores of all the groups indicate that the biological teachers, irrespective of their gender and experience are moderate. The variations in the scores on different aspects of biological science textbook, as revealed from the standard deviations, are also not high. The Table given below indicates about the rating of evaluation of textbook on different aspects.

Table 4.18: *Rating of Textbook on Different Aspects*

S. No.	*Statement*	*High*	*Moderate*	*Low*
1	Physical aspects of Biological Science Textbook of Class IX			√
2	Printing quality		√	
3	Representation of content	√		
4	Organization of content		√	
5	Figures, graphs and tables			√
6	Homework, assignment and self-study materials		√	
7	Reference material		√	
8	At the end of each unit appropriate summary helping in increasing the understanding for the unit	√		
9	The Examples contained in the book is enough to strengthen the student's understanding of the biological concept	√		
10	Possibility of having variety of teaching methods in teaching biology in Class IX		√	
11	The proposed activities are reliable and possible to do	√		
12	Learning outcomes are not specified			√
13	Possibility of laboratory work.		√	

From the above Table it is observed that majority of the science teachers opined on physical aspects of Biological Science Textbook of Class IX are not satisfactory on account of the size of the textbook, binding of the book and quality of paper. Most of the respondents were of the opinion that the printing quality of the book is moderate on the points though the printing is clear but not attractive, letters are not of proper size, small and capital letters are not used appropriately, printing in two columns made it easier in reading but use of more colour must give attractive look to the textbook of biological science. From the table it is studied that majority of the science teachers supported the representation of the content which is easily understandable, some mistakes are there in punctuation marks and spellings, language and wordings of the content is not according to the age of students, content is not enough for the formative and summative assessment, introduction and summary is useful for students, definitions are clearly presented, more examples are given to clarify the content, scientific terms are not easily understandable, few of the scientific terms are mentioned in English, syllabus is lengthy according to examination, presentation of terms and symbols are not uniform, selection of content is not according to educational objective and content is not presented in logical sequence.

From the Table it is confirmed that majority of the respondents were of view on organization of content is moderate on the basis of opinions that the aim of textbook is suitable for mental capability of the students, study of content is useful to develop scientific attitude, helpful to teacher for using effective methods of teaching, principles, concepts, formulas, examples and experiments are realistic, content is organized as per psychological point of view, activities and additional information is used to clarify content, content is consistent with textbook, examples are co-related with real life but the respondents are agreed on the statement content is not co-related with daily life, enough weightage is not given on required topic.

From the Table it is observed and analyzed that the respondents were of opinion that figures, graphs and tables are not up to the mark, pictures and figures are not of proper size, more figures and tables are not given in experiments, but figures are given on proper places and more pictures are provided in the textbook.

As per the study of above Table it is seen that maximum respondents were of opinion that homework, assignment and self-study were of moderate level, the questions for self-study were given at the end of every chapter, all topics have been provided with evaluation questions/ exercise, every type of questions is provided in exercises. Answers to every question can be found within content, self-study questions, format of questions are not proper, exercises are useful to enhance self-study, questions are not repeated and questions are framed properly and are free from ambiguity.

From the Table it is inferred that majority of the respondents opined that the reference material is moderate on the basis of the book, has not cited appropriate number of reference science books for teachers and students, alphabetical index is not given, reference material is not given after every chapter, proper guidance for use of textbook is not given, exercises are not lengthy, deep understanding of experimental was not given, enough synonyms for scientific term should be given, glossary is not sufficient and website address is not given in all chapters.

From this table maximum science teachers observed that in the statement on the end of each unit appropriate summary helping in increasing the understanding for the unit is highly appreciated.

From the table it is minutely observed that majority of the respondents highly recommended on the statement that the examples contained in the book are enough to strengthen the student's understanding of the biological concept. From the above study it is found that majority of the science teachers the possibility of having variety of teaching methods in teaching the biology in Class IX viewed moderate on this context.

The table speaks about the majority of respondents opined on the context the proposed activities are reliable and it is possible to do is favoured highly. This table confirmed on the heading of learning outcomes are not specified but majority of the respondents clearly viewed it is low. From the table it is observed on the heading possibility of laboratory work moderate importance given by the respondents.

Evaluation of Biological Science Textbook of Class IX on the Basis of Responses of Experts

Objective No. 5: To examine the opinions of experts on various aspects of Biological Science Textbook of Class IX

General Profile of Experts

Table 4.19: *General profile of Experts*

S. No.	*Profile*	*Category*	*No*	*%*
1	Gender	Male	06	60
		Female	04	40
2	Educational Qualification	M.Sc. B.Ed.	01	10
		M.Sc. M.Ed.	04	40
		Ph.D.	05	50
3	Experience	Above 10 years	06	60
		Below 10 Years	04	40

The above table speaks about the general profile of the experts. From the Table it is seen that 60 per cent of the experts are male and 40 per cent are female. With regards to qualification of the experts, 10 per cent are M.Sc. B.Ed., 40 per cent are M.Sc. M.Ed. and 50 per cent are having Ph.D. qualification. Similarly, 60 per cent experts are having above 10 years of teaching experience and 40 per cent are below 10 years of teaching experience. The graphical representations are given below.

Opinion of Experts on Biological Science Textbook of Class IX

In order to know the opinion of experts about the various aspects of Biological Science Textbook data has been collected and presented in the following Table.

Table 4.20: *Opinion of Experts on Different aspects of Biological Science Textbook*

S. No.	Statements	Agreed (%)	Disagree (%)	Undecided (%)
1.	Overall physical features of the book are satisfactory	70	30	00
2.	Contents of the book are properly arranged	60	40	00
3.	Examples from the local culture has been cited	30	70	00
4.	Difficulty level of contents in the Book Neither too difficult nor too easy	90	10	00
5.	Illustrations in the book are satisfactory	70	30	00
6.	Quality and sufficiency of exercises in the book are satisfactory	90	10	00
7.	Practical work/activities has been given in the book	60	30	10
8.	Developing scientific skills among the students has been cited	60	30	10
9.	Ample opportunities for Laboratory work have been given.	70	30	00

From the above Table it is found that 70 per cent of the experts are agreed to the statement that physical feature of the book is satisfactory, 60 per cent experts are satisfied that the contents of the book are properly arranged, 30 per cent agreed with the statement of examples from the local culture has been cited whereas, difficulty level of contents in the book is neither too difficult nor too easy are agreed by 90 per cent of the experts.

With regards to illustration of the book 70 per cent experts are satisfied, 90 per cent are agreed about the quality and sufficiency of exercises in the book, 60 per cent are agreed to the practical work/ activities has been given in the book and developing scientific skills among the students has been cited and 70 per cent experts agreed ample opportunities for Laboratory work have been given in the Biological Science Textbook of Class IX of BSE, Odisha.

Physical Features of this Book

From the above table 70 per cent of the experts were of the view that the physical features of the book are not up to the mark, be it cover page, pictures displayed on the cover page, printing of the book, pictures displayed on different pages of the book, quality of the paper used, binding of the book, water mark etc. The experts seem to be satisfied with other physical features of the book like font size, font style, line spacing, price, weight, size and number of pages in the book.

Assessment about the Contents of the Book

Majority (60 per cent) of the experts were of the view that the contents in the book are according to the mental maturity of the students. Majority (70 per cent) of the experts were of the view that examples have not been taken from local culture wherever possible. Most (90 per cent) of the experts were of the view that Scientific names of Plants and Animals have been properly written. The experts were of the view that the introduction of the chapters is very brief. The experts were also of the view that the work done by teachers will help the students to practice at the home. Moreover, they were of the view that there are certain contents in different chapters of the book which have been narrowly discussed for which a teacher has to use supplementary material to make them understand to students. They were also of the view that the contents in the current science textbook do not find any link to the contents covered in Class VIII Science textbook. The experts were also of the view that the contents in the book have not been systematically placed.

Difficulty Level of Contents in the Book

Most (90 per cent) of the experts were of the view that the contents in the book are neither too difficult nor too easy which is pre-requisite of a good textbook. However, there are certain chapters in the book which students will find difficult. Out of 10 experts, three were of the view that the contents in the book are moderate, one is of the view that the contents are difficult and six were of the view that the contents are easy.

Illustrations in the Book

Majority (70 per cent) of the experts were of the view that the illustrations in the book are up to the mark. However, there are certain topics/places in the book where illustrations could have been taken from the state of Odisha which are missing. About 40 per cent of the experts rate the illustrations 7 out of 10 and only 10 per cent experts rate about 6 and 8. A very negligible percentage of teachers rate the book on 9 i.e., extremely difficult. Out of 10 experts, the ratings for illustrations were: 10 Extremely Difficult, 09 Very Difficult, 08 Pretty Difficult, 07 Mildly Difficult, 06 Slightly Difficult, 05 Neutral, 04 Slightly Easy, 03 Mildly Easy, 02 Pretty Easy, 01 Very Easy.

Table 4.21: *Difficulty Level of Content in the Book as Viewed by the Experts*

Rating Points	*Frequency (No. of Experts)*	*Percentage*
1-5	Nil	0
6	1	10
7	4	40
8	3	30
9	2	20
10	Nil	0

Quality and Sufficiency of Exercises in the Book

Most (90 per cent) of the experts were of the opinion that the exercises at the end of the lesson are of diversified nature touching different aspects of different domains. Majority (70 per cent) of the experts were of the view that In-Text questions should have been presented from unit First onwards. Most of the experts were of the view that In-Text questions are not enough in the book. Questions on Higher Order Thinking Skills (HOTS) are not given in the textbook. Exercises at the end of the lesson are sufficient and student friendly. Key words and summary at the end of the lesson makes it easier for students to recapitulate the lesson. Extending learning activities help them in gaining more information about the different topics/concepts. Websites at the end of the lesson provide them with readymade material for a particular concept and are often used as a supplementary material to broaden their vision regarding a particular concept.

Contents of the Book in Relation to the State of Odisha

Most (70 per cent) of the experts were of the view that there are certain contents in the book which are related to Odisha. However, there is not a single chapter in the book which is wholly and solely devoted to the state. Moreover, certain pictures related to different concepts could have been taken from the local culture to make the book more comfortable and interesting for the students.

Practical Work/Activities in the Book as per NEP 2020

Majority (60 per cent) of the experts are of the view that there are too many activities for the explanation of a single concept which sometimes dilutes the meaning of concept in the book. But on the other hand, practical work/ activities in the book have been taken due care. New ways of doing different things have been introduced so as to make the students creative in their approach of doing different things.

Developing Scientific Skills among the Students

Most (80 per cent) of the experts were of the view that there is enough content in the book which will develop scientific temper among the students. Moreover, they were of the view that students should be made habitual of observing different biological terms scientific phenomenon on scientific lines instead of believing in myths. The language used in the textbooks is authentic, clear and ambiguous. The progression of figures and symbols is appropriate. The scientific concepts are presented with brief and easy examples and explanations in textbooks, but the functions of the concepts do not exemplify their future use.

Laboratory Work

Most (70 per cent) of the experts were of the view that it should be spelt out about the laboratory work in the biological science textbook of Class IX. Enough laboratory work should be incorporated in the book. The book is lacking practical activities. Moreover, they were of the view that students should be made habitual of biology laboratory. Individual and group work should be highlighted.

Strength and Weaknesses of Biological Science Textbook

Objective No. 6: To analyze the opinions of biological science teachers on strengths and weaknesses of Biological Science Textbook of Class IX as per NEP 2020

There are many strengths and weaknesses of the biological science textbook of Class IX of BSE, Odisha. The researcher collected information about the strength and weakness of the biological science textbook of Class IX from the FGDs among the teachers. The researcher conducted three FGDs in different blocks which has described in Chapter III. The summary of the FGDs regarding strength and weakness of the biological science textbook analyzed under.

Strength of the Biological Science Textbook

From all the FGDs it is found that the Content coverage is according to the prescribed syllabus by the Board of Secondary Education, Odisha. The books cover all the objectives of Board of Secondary Education, Odisha, and it is as per the guideline of NCF-2005 and SCF-2007. The subject matter is adequately selected through various topics and sub-topics. Standard symbols and abbreviations are used. The textbook contains three aspects i.e., text, cognitive strategies and implication for practice. Subject matter presented in the textbooks are easy and lucid to understand and followed the principle of simple to complex pattern. Similarly, the subject matter in biological science textbook is selective, sequential and coherent in terms of the ability, maturity and interests of the learners. The selection of the topic will enhance the 21st century skills among the secondary school students of Odisha.

It is found that from the FGDs, the cover of the Biological Science Textbook of Class IX was appropriate and the picture on cover page was attractive. The content was designed according to the psychological requirements of the students and on the other hand should serve the purpose of the teacher as well who wishes to impart the knowledge in an interesting manner. As per the views of teachers the selection of contents were as per the need, ability and mental maturity of the learners.

From all the FGDs it is found that the examples contained in the Biological Science Textbook of Class IX are enough to strengthen the student's understanding of the biological concept. It is found that there is enough content in the book which will develop scientific temper among the students. The proposed activities in the textbook are reliable and possible to do. Most of the participants of the FGD were of the opinion that the exercises at the end of the lesson are of diversified nature touching different aspects of different domains.

Most of the sections are for average students and a few topics within the sections or a few sections are for above-average students. One of the teachers said that "Demonstration and Problem-solving aspect of the method of teaching is stressed. The authors' style of writing is informal and interesting. Important laws/principles are given in italics or bold face. Summaries, questions and exercises/activities at the end of the chapters are adequate" It is found that majority of the biological science teachers opined that the variety of teaching methods in teaching Biology in Class IX is possible. Most of the teachers opined that integration of contemporary subjects like holistic health, organic living, environmental education which is highlighted in NEP 2020 in Biological Science Textbook is adequate for Class IX students.

Weakness of Biological Science Textbook of Class IX as per National Education Policy 2020

From the FGDs it was found that most of the teachers opined that the paper used in the book was not good. The size of the book was not perfect. Binding of the book is not durable. The learning objectives and learning outcomes are missing in the textbook. The topics and sub-topics were not selected properly but they opined that examples should be from the local environment and style and culture of the people. The book is not commensurate with a modern scientific development. Most of the teachers opined that the examples contained in the book are not enough to strengthen the student's understanding of the scientific material.

Most of the respondents in the FGD highlighted that the biological science book of Class IX had adequate content but some more explanation in some units and readjustments in some units were necessary. There is a sudden introduction of new ideas of so many concepts without relating to previous concepts are found in the textbook. Thus, the subject matter is not articulated. Participants emphasized that the textbook is encouraged by rote and the teachers could use it as a reference book. At the same time, they think that the textbook was not designed according to any of the learning theories and so does not lead to durable learning. Similarly, most of the teachers pointed out that all the illustrations in the textbook are black and white.

In the FGDs it was found that almost all the teachers said that verbal explanations in the biological science textbook of Class IX are not very clear. Some places it creates confusions only to the students. There are no puzzles and riddles in the textbook. No doubt there are multiple choice questions, very short questions, short answer questions and essay type questions measuring knowledge, understanding, application and skill. Diagnostic evaluation, remedial and enrichment programmes are absent.

The Biological Science Textbook of Class IX lacks pedagogical consideration for organizing the textbook, reference material is not provided in the textbook, and bibliography is absent in the textbook was said by the respondents in the FGD. Most of the respondents said that not a single chapter in the book contains URL(s) as they are helpful in gaining additional knowledge about the different concepts in the book.

Most of the teachers highlighted in the FGD that biological science textbook lacks field-based activities and experiments so as to promote creative and independent thinking among the students. The textbook also lacks local content and flavour as highlighted by NEP 2020. The book is silent about the biological science project and laboratory work. Most of the respondents in the FGD said that the biological science textbook of Class IX lacks ICT integration and modern gadgets.

Measures for the Improvement of Class IX Biological Science Textbook

Objectve No. 7: To examine the opinions of biological science teachers and experts on suggestions to improve the Biological Science Textbook of Class IX as per NEP 2020

Table 4.22: *Opinion of Secondary School Teachers and Experts on Suggestions to Improve the Biological Science Textbook of Class IX*

S. No.	*Suggestions*	*Teachers (%)*	*Experts (%)*
1.	Physical features of the book need to be improved	75	80
2.	Difficulty level of some units of the book needs to be reassessed	72	60
3.	Contents need to be arranged systematically	79	40
4.	Contents should be more interesting, motivating and challenging	52	60
5.	field-based activities and experiments should be made so as to promote creative and independent thinking among the students.	69	60
6.	Different scientific phenomenon should be explained	64	60
7.	Current issues in biological science should find a place in its next revised edition	93	90
8.	ICT should find a place in the book	75	90
9.	Local examples should find a place exclusively in the book	59	50
10.	More activities should be included in the biological science textbook	77	70
11.	More homework must be given in the science textbook	71	70
12.	Project work should be included in few topics along with names of journals and popular science magazines	72	70
13.	More number of questions from knowledge, understanding, application and skills should be included	73	60
14.	More number of simple examples from daily experiences should be cited in each topic	75	60
15.	Questions on HOTS should be included in the textbook	71	60
16.	Due importance may be given for all types of learners	74	70

From the above Table the following suggestions were derived for the improvement of the Biological Science Textbook of Class IX of BSE, Odisha. About 75 per cent of the respondents' said that physical features of the book need to be improved. Reassessment of difficulty level of some units in the book viewed by 72 per cent of teachers and 60 per cent of experts. About 79 per cent of teachers and 40 per cent of experts viewed contents need to be arranged systematically. Content should be made more interesting, motivating and challenging, viewed by 52 per cent of teachers and 60 per cent of experts.

About 69 per cent of teachers and 60 per cent of experts said that provision for more field-based activities and experiments should be made so as to promote creative and independent thinking among the students. Attachment of CD explaining different scientific phenomenon may prove beneficial to students and teachers viewed by 64 per cent of teachers and 60 per cent of experts. Continuity among the chapters belonging to a particular field viewed by 72 per cent of teachers and 60 per cent of experts. Current issues in biological science should find a place in its next revised edition viewed by 93 per cent of teachers and 90 per cent of experts.

ICT should find a place in the book. The use of modern gadgets should find a place as well in the book viewed by 75 per cent of teachers and 90 per cent of experts. Few topics related to the state of Odisha (local examples) should find a place exclusively in the book viewed by 59 per cent of teachers and 50 per cent of experts. More activities should be included in the Biological Science Textbook viewed by 77 per cent of teachers and 70 per cent of experts.

More homework must be given in the science textbook viewed by 71 per cent of teachers and 70 per cent of experts. Some project work should be included in few topics along with names of journals and popular science magazines so that reading habits and collaborative learning skills may be developed, viewed by 72 per cent of teachers and 70 per cent of experts.

More number of questions from knowledge, understanding, application and skills should be included at the end of each chapter, viewed by 73 per cent of teachers and 60 per cent of experts. More number of simple examples from daily experiences should be cited in each topic, viewed by 75 per cent of teachers and 60 per cent of experts.

Questions on HOTS (Higher-order thinking) should be included in the textbook, viewed by 71 per cent of teachers and 60 per cent of experts. Due importance may be given to all types of learners — dull, mediocre brilliant, and rural and urban communities, viewed by 74 per cent of teachers and 70 per cent of experts.

Discussions

The primary function of the cover page is to save the interior pages from damaging, but it was found that the cover page of the book is weak and is not hard enough so that it can withstand the whole session for the students. Thus, cover pages lose their primary essence. Pictures displayed on its cover page seem to be appropriate as they reflect certain themes/concepts related to science. Pictures displayed on different pages of the book are not up to the mark as well. The quality of pictures used in the book is extremely poor as most of them are blurred. Moreover, the quality of ink used in the pictures is below standard and of low quality. There is a famous proverb, "A Picture Speaks Thousand Words" but unfortunately the pictures in the book can prove to be counter-productive. The findings of the study are similar to the findings of many authors. (Hamid H and Al-Rubaie1 Yusef Faleh Muhammad Al-Saadi, 2021, Patel, A., 2009, Kanaiyalal, D., 2007, Oishi, A., 2020, Garinger, 2000 and Miekley. 2005, Zubair, A. et al., 2020, Riasati and Zare, 2010, Vijay B., 2008, Kumkum, M., and Rani, A, 2019)

The paper used for the book is not of good quality as the paper doesn't look neat and clean and looks like recycled paper has been used for the book. The book is not securely bound, the pages of the book come off after using it for 20 to 25 days. Water mark in the book makes it difficult for the readers to read and understand the words properly at certain places. However, there are other physical features of the book with whom majority of the experts agree that they are up to the mark and needs no revision. Which is font size, font style, line spacing, price, weight, size and number of pages in the book is up to the mark. On reviewing the book by investigator, it was found that 14 font size has been used in the book throughout which does not strain the eyes of the readers be it students or teachers and is readable by all ages. Line spacing seems to be 1.5 throughout the book barring a few places where line spacing is 1.0. The price of the book is Rs. 30 which is reasonable and is not a burden on the pocket, weight of the book is appropriate as well, on weighing machine its weight was found to be around 300 grams. The size of the book is perfect according to experts. The book is not lengthy in terms of pages as well as the responses from the experts suggest the same. The findings of the study are similar to the findings of many authors. (Hamid H and Al-Rubaiel Yusef Faleh Muhammad Al-Saadi 2021, Patel, A., 2009, Kanaiyalal, D., 2007, Oishi, A., 2020, Garinger, 2000 and Miekley, 2005, Zubair, A. et al., 2020, Riasati and Zare, 2010, Vijay B, 2008, Kumkum, M., and Rani, A., 2019)

Most of the experts were of the view that examples from Odisha should have been taken wherever possible for the explanation of different concepts. Some concepts in the book have been narrowly discussed, introduction of the chapters is brief, scientific names of plants and animals have been properly written in the book. However, supplementary material is required for various concepts/contents in the book. The findings of the study are similar to the findings of many authors. (Hamid H and Al-Rubaiel Yusef Faleh Muhammad Al-Saadi 2021, Patel, A., 2009, Kanaiyalal, D., 2007, Oishi, A., 2020, Garinger, 2000 and Miekley)

On revision of the book, the researcher found that the chapters in the book have not been sequentially arranged as they do not follow simple to complex pattern. Moreover, the chapters in the book have been haphazardly placed, not maintaining any proper order. Moreover, there are certain topics in the book which have been briefly discussed.

The findings of the study say that the book is according to the mental maturity of the students. However, as the data gathered from teachers show that there are certain chapters in the book which experts and teachers find difficult. The result of the study is very similar to the studies conducted by Hamid H and Al-Rubaiel Yusef Faleh Muhammad Al-Saadi 2021, Patel, A., 2009, Kanaiyalal, D., 2007, Oishi, A., 2020, Garinger, 2000 and Miekley, 2005, Zubair, A., et al., 2020, Riasati and Zare, 2010, Vijay, B.,2008, Kumkum, M., and Rani, A., 2019 Pai, J., 1997, Joshi, J., 1990, Patel, L., 1997, and Suthar, B., 2009.

It is found that the exercises at the end of the lesson are of diversified nature touching different aspects of different domains. The majority of the experts were of the view that In-Text questions should have been presented from unit First onwards. Most of the experts were of the view that In-Text questions are not enough in the book.

Majority of the experts and teachers were of the view that Exercises at the end of the lesson are not sufficient and student friendly. Most of the respondents were of the view that key words and summary at the end of the lesson makes it easier for students to recapitulate the lesson but key words are not copacetic. These findings are very common to the findings of the study of Hamid H and Al-Rubaiel Yusef Faleh Muhammad Al-Saadi 2021, Patel, A., 2009, Kanaiyalal, D., 2007, Oishi, A., 2020, Garinger, 2000 and Miekley, 2005, Zubair, A., et al., 2020, Riasati and Zare, 2010, Vijay, B.,2008, Kumkum, M., and Rani, A., 2019, Pai, J., 1997, Joshi, J., 1990, Patel, L. 1997, and Suthar, B., 2009.

The findings of the study reveal that Websites at the end of the lesson are not provided to find ready-made material for a particular concept and are often used as a supplementary material to broaden their vision regarding a particular concept (Zubair, A. et al., 2020, Riasati and Zare, 2010, Vijay, B., 2008, Kumkum, M., and Rani, A., 2019). The findings also show that mixed type of questions touch the different aspects of Blooms Taxonomy. The above findings are in the line of the findings of Hamid H and Al- Rubaiel Yusef Faleh Muhammad Al-Saadi 2021, Patel, A., 2009, Kanaiyalal, D., 2007, Oishi, A., 2020, Garinger, 2000 and Miekley, 2005, Pai, J., 1997, Joshi, J 1990, Patel, L., 1997, Suthar, B., 2009, Mohd. F and Mohd. A, 2017, Eugene, L., Chiappetta and David, A., Fillman, 2008 and Sharma, R., 2016.

It was found that there are sufficient illustrations in the book to make understand different concepts to the students. Examples have not been taken from local environment wherever possible which makes it easier to difficult for students to understand a particular concept, Mohd. F and Mohd. A 2017, Eugene, L., Chiappetta and David, A., Fillman, 2008 and NCERT, 2016.

There are adequate exercises at the end of the lesson. Questions are of mixed nature ranging from short answer, long answer, matching type, fill in the blank, word puzzle, true false, one word substitution, etc. Thus, there is a dire need to keep the in-text questions which will enable a teacher to know the progress of his students on a weekly basis. Furthermore, it was found that at the end of the lesson key words are not given. Summary at the end of the lesson is well maintained in each and every chapter which makes it easier for students to recapitulate the whole lesson within no time. These findings are also similar to the findings of Garinger, 2000 and Miekley, 2005, Pai, J., 1997, Joshi, J., 1990, Patel, L., 1997, Suthar, B., 2009. Mohd. F and Mohd. A, 2017. It is found that ICT and use of modern gadgets should find a place in the book. These findings are very similar to the findings of Patel, M., 2017 who also emphasized the inclusion of ICT component in the Biological Science Textbook. Extending learning activities are also not present in every chapter which will develop scientific skills among students as they have to perform different kinds of activities based on different objectives. It was found that the practical work/ activities in the book are according to the mental level of average and above average students. Slow learners /below average students will be facing a lot of problems while performing different activities.

V

Improving Science Textbooks

Suggestions and Educational Implications

The present study was undertaken to study the opinion of secondary school biological science teachers on various aspects of biological science textbook prescribed by Board of Secondary Education, Odisha. Data has been analyzed and interpreted. In this chapter attempt has been made to present the findings, Summary and educational implications of the study systemically.

Major Findings

1. About 70 per cent teachers and 80 per cent experts were of the view that the textbook had been prepared as per the guiding principle of NCF 2005 and SCF 2007.
2. The biological science textbook of Class IX was appropriate to develop scientific aptitude and skills required for 21st century was supported by 87 per cent of biological science teachers and 70 per cent of experts.
3. About (75 per cent) of the teachers and experts (70 per cent) were of the view that cover page, pictures on cover page, pictures on different pages are not attractive and binding of the textbook of Class IX is not enough tight whereas price of the book is affordable.
4. Most of the respondents 64 per cent teachers and 70 per cent experts were of the view that paper quality and binding of the book is not up to the mark. Whereas most of the teachers (74 per cent) were of the view that the font size, font style, line spacing, price, weight, size and number of pages in the book are up to the mark.
5. There is no difference of opinion Class IX of BSE, Odisha of teachers having teaching experience of more than 10 years and less than ten years.
6. The printing quality of the biological science textbook of Class IX was not clean and clear viewed by 79 per cent of the teachers and 70 per cent of the experts. Whereas about (75 per cent) of the teachers viewed that the letters in the textbook are of proper size. Similarly, 74 per cent of the biological science teachers

agreed on printing in two columns made reading easier. About (63 per cent) of the teachers agreed that use of more than one colour makes printing effective.

7. The presentation of content is easily understandable expressed by (79 per cent) of the teachers and 70 per cent of experts. With respect to language and wordings content designed as per the age of students are not agreed by most of the respondents and only 21 per cent science teachers agreed to that statement.
8. Most of the respondents (72 per cent) agreed that the aim of textbook is suitable for mental capability of students and a few disagreed with the statement. Most of the biological science teachers (82 per cent) and experts (60 per cent) agreed that the content is organized according to the psychological point of view of students of the age group.
9. About (67 per cent) of the science teachers were of the view on the study of content is useful to develop scientific attitude. Whereas 75 per cent of the respondents agreed that the content is not co-related with daily life. Similarly, about 89 per cent of the respondents agreed on the principles, concepts, formulas, examples and experiments are realistic.
10. For effective methods of teaching 94 per cent of the science teachers are of the view that the textbook is helpful whereas 49 per cent of the respondents agreed on the context of enough weightage is given on required topics as per the present needs of the society.
11. About 70 per cent of experts and 78 per cent teachers were also of the view that the contents in the Biological Science Textbook do not find any link to the contents covered in Class VIII Science textbook.
12. Activities, laboratory work in biological science, examples co-related with real life, and additional information in the Biological Science Textbook of Class IX are useful to clarify the content viewed by 74 per cent of the science teachers and 70 per cent of the experts. About 70 per cent experts and teachers are of the opinion that examples have not been taken from local culture wherever possible
13. There is a difference between the opinions about organization of content of Biological Science Textbook of under ten years teaching experience and above ten years teaching experience science teachers of Odisha at .05 level of significance. The hostile gain scores favour below ten years teaching experience teachers.

14. With regards to figures, graphs and tables about 67 per cent of the science teachers and 60 per cent of experts agreed that enough figures are given in the textbook but not of proper size.
15. About 95 per cent of the biological science teachers and 80 per cent of experts gave satisfactory view that the figures are given on proper places with nomenclature to clarify the content.
16. With respect to homework, assignment and self-study materials, 60 per cent of teachers and 70 per cent experts are of the view that questions for self-study are given at the end of every chapter in the Biological Science Textbook. Whereas almost all the teachers (150 in number) agreed that enough objective type questions and questions on HOTS are not given in the textbook.
17. There is no difference between the teachers' opinions about homework, assignment, self-study materials and reference material of below ten years teaching experience or even more than ten years teaching experience secondary school science teachers of Odisha.
18. About 78 per cent biological science teachers and 70 per cent experts are of the view that Biological Science Textbook of Class IX has not cited appropriate number of reference books and alphabetical index for teachers and students. Similarly, all the respondents agreed that website addresses are not given in the chapters of Biological Science Textbook of Class IX.
19. The strength of this book viewed by experts and biological science teachers. The book has been prepared as per guidelines of NCF 2005 and SCF 2007 and fulfils the objectives framed by Board of Secondary Education, Odisha but the weaknesses of the book are that it should be arranged sequentially topic and sub-topic should be explained with more examples and it will be from the day to day life.
20. As per the suggestions of all science teachers and experts agreed that the said textbook should be revised and lessons should be presented with more practical activity with ICT materials, current issues and modern gadgets.

Suggestions for Improvement

The most common feedback received from the respondents are summarized below:

1. Physical features of the book need to be improved.
2. Reassessment of difficulty level of some units in the book.

3. Contents need to be arranged systematically.
4. Content should be made more interesting, motivating and challenging.
5. Indian knowledge system will be included in Biological Science Textbook.
6. Provision for more field-based activities and experiments should be made so as to promote creative and independent thinking among the students.
7. Attachment of CD explaining different scientific phenomenon may prove beneficial to students and teachers.
8. Continuity among the chapters belonging to a particular field.
9. Current issues in biological science should find a place in its next revised edition.
10. ICT and use of modern gadgets should find a place in the book.
11. A Few topics related to the state of Odisha should find an exclusive place in the book.
12. More activities should be included in the Biological Science Textbook.
13. More homework must be given in the science textbook.
14. Some project work should be included in a few topics along with names of journals and popular science magazines so that reading habits and collaborative learning skills may be developed.
15. More number of questions from knowledge, understanding, application and skills should be included at the end of each chapter.
16. More number of simple examples from daily experiences should be cited in each topic.
17. Questions on HOTS should also be included in the textbook.
18. Due importance to be given for all types of learners — dull, mediocre and brilliant, rural and urban communities.

Educational Implications

The findings of the study have the implications for students, teachers and experts as well as for curriculum planners. Thus, it has wide educational implications for enhancing the quality of the Biological Science Textbook of Class IX of BSE, Odisha in particular and any textbook in general.

A: Implications for Students

There is a direct implication for students about the quality of the textbooks. The textbook is a learning tool for students thus a good

Biological Science Textbook would help the students to enhance their learning and to develop scientific enquiry. The price of the textbook should be less so that they can afford. The get-up should be attractive, binding should be durable, printing quality should be clear, picture should be colourful, illustrations and examples should be appropriate. Hence, Biological Science Textbook prescribed by BSE, Odisha should be improved. The objectives of all the lessons should be clearly stated in the said book and the content should be arranged accordingly. The present study will help the students to read the textbook as a learning tool.

B: Implications for Textbook Writers

While writing textbook experienced teachers and experts should be involved. From their experience they should select the appropriate units in the subjects with proper examples, arrange the unit and sub-unit by following the principles of learning simple to complex, particular to general, known to unknown. The lessons should be arranged on as per the age, ability and mental maturity of students. Examples and illustrations should be given at the end of the chapter's summary. Further, assignments and glossary should find in proper place. Ample opportunities should be given for practical work. Activity-based approach should be used for designing the lessons of the book. This study will help the textbook writers to follow the above findings while preparing the Biological Science Textbook.

C: Implications for Biological Science Teachers

A textbook is a teaching tool of biological science teachers. He should go through the book before coming to class. He should be fully aware of the instructional objectives of the lessons, should organize the teaching points and learning outcomes. It helps the teacher to give home assignments to his students. It helps him to set questions papers. It is essential for biology course to make experiments and activities in laboratory. Teachers can create an environment so that students can feel as if they work like scientists in the laboratories.

The present study would help her to go through all this process. Her feedback will provide guidance to rectify the weaknesses of the book. After recommendation of NCF 2005 and the textbook should be edited, improved and aware about the process of science teaching as per the guiding principles of NPE 1986 and NPE 2020. The study will help the teachers to conduct their own action type research for improving textbook in other subjects also. The present study is to plan her teaching learning activities in a better way.

D: Textbook Publishers

Both Publishers and Board of Secondary Education, Odisha will benefit by knowing the physical and academic aspect of textbook and errors and suggestions for the improvement of the textbooks. They can modify the textbooks accordingly in the next edition of the book.

Suggestions for Further Study

Although the investigator attempted to carry on her investigation in a scientific and objective manner, it would not be fair to state that the study was ideal or was free from errors. There were many limitations of the study and there is ample scope for follow-up and further research in this field. If these limitations are done away with, future research would show better results. The following topic or refinements indicate the directions and priorities that future research in the area might take for its scientific verifications and proper generalizations. On the basis of the findings and experience of the present study, the following suggestions are made for the further research in this area:

1. The present investigation attempted to evaluate biology textbooks of high school classes. It would be worthwhile to attempt to conduct research on the textbooks of other subjects at high school level.
2. The present study was conducted at the high school level. An institutional study can be carried out on the textbooks of science from Class VI to X of Odisha.
3. Hierarchical studies can be conducted on all the school subjects.
4. A Similar study can be conducted by increasing the number of tools and evaluators.
5. Empirical studies can be carried out for better objectives results.
6. Opinions from educational professionals, writers, college professors may also be gathered and analyzed.
7. A comparative study of old and new science textbook may be done.
8. A comparative study of science textbooks of two neighbour state may also be done.

Conclusion

The present research was to study the opinion of secondary teachers on various aspects of Biological Science Textbook of Class IX in the academic session 2019-20 prescribed by Board of Secondary

Education, Odisha. The textbook has been prepared after NCF 2005 and SCF 2007. No opinion study has been done in Odisha. The NPE 1986 and NPE 2020 stress much on importance of teaching for developing scientific aptitudes and acquisition of various skills needed for 21st century. The strength and weakness of the Biological Science Textbook of Class IX would help, teachers, textbook publishers, writers, curriculum planners and editors related with Class IX biological science subjects to modify the textbook accordingly.

The researcher hopes that the textbook would be revised accordingly which would help all science teachers in general and biological science teachers in particular to perform their duties in a most meaningful manner. The present study, no doubt, has many limitations. The findings of the study would definitely help to improve the Biological Science Textbook of Class IX of secondary school Odisha. If the textbook of Biological Science Textbook is improved, our schools can produce good scientists who can surely shape the destiny of India in future.

Bibilography

Agrawal, J. C. (1966). *Educational Research: An Introduction*, New Delhi: Arya Book Depot.

Ahmadi, A., & Derakhshan, A. (2015). An evaluation of the Iranian junior high school English textbooks "Prospect1" and its old version "Right Path to English1" from teachers' perceptions, *International Journal of English Language and Literature Studies, 4*(1), 37-48.

Ahmadi, A., & Derakhshan, A. (2016). EFL teachers' perceptions towards textbook evaluation. *Theory and Practice in Language Studies*, 6(2), 260-267.

Ahmed, F., & Narcy-Combes, M.F. (2011). An analysis of textbooks from a cultural. *TESOL Journal,* 5, 21-37.

Ahour, T., & Ahmadi, E. (2012). Retrospective evaluation of textbook "Summit 2B" for its suitability for EFL undergraduate students. Book of Proceedings of the International Conference on Human and Social Sciences, 6, 176-184.

Ahour, T., Towhidian., B., & Saeidi, M. (2013). The evaluation of "English textbook 2" taught in Iranian high schools from teachers' perspectives. *English Language Teaching,* 7(3), 150-158.

Ajda, K. (2010). Quantitative analysis of Science and Chemistry textbooks for indicators of reform: A complementary perspective, *International Journal of Science Education*, 32(11), 1495-1519, DOI: 10.1080/09500690903127649

Alaghaa, F., Farajollahib, M., & Shahmohammadi, N. (2014). The content analysis of the experimental Science book of second grade of guidance school based on the amount of attention to the areas of creativity and implementing with Guilford's mental exercise. Procedia — Social and Behavioural Sciences.

Ali, M. M. (2017). An evaluation of 'English for today: For classes 11-12' as a textbook for Bangladesh Higher Secondary Education. *The English Teacher*, (1), 18.

Ali, M., & Walker, A.L. (2014). Bogged down ELT in Bangladesh: Problems and policy: Investigating some problems that encumber ELT in an EFL context. *English Today*, 30(2), 33-38.

Alshumaimeri, Y.A., & Alzyadi, M.S. (2015). Using material authenticity in the Saudi English textbook design: A content analysis from the viewpoint of EFL teachers. *Advances in Language and Literary Studies*, 6(2), 229-241.

Ann, G.E., (2004). Science textbooks for lower secondary schools in Brunei: Issues of gender equity, *International Journal of Science Education*, 26(7), 875-894

Arriassecq, I., & Greco, I. M. (2007). Approaches to the teaching of special relativity theory in high school and university textbooks of Argentina, *Science and Education* 16, 65–86.

Awasthi, J.R. (2006). Textbook and its evaluation. *Journal of NELTA*, 11(1-2), 1-10.

Azam, A., & Ali, D. (2016). EFL teachers' perceptions towards textbook evaluation. *Theory and Practice in Language Studies, 6(2), 260-267,* DOI: http://dx.doi.org/10.17507/tpls.0602.06

Azizfar, A. (2009). An analytical evaluation of Iranian high school: ELT textbooks from 1970 to 2010. *The Journal of Applied Linguistics*, 2(2), 52-79.

Babaei, B. & Abdi, A. (2014). Textbooks content analysis of social studies and natural sciences of secondary school based on emotional intelligence components. *Universal Journal of Educational Research,* 2(4), 309-325, retrieved from http://www.hrpub.org

Bakulchanda, J.S. (2009). A critical study of Science and Technology textbook of standard-10 of Gujarat state. Jain Vishvabharati Vishvavidyalay, Ladnoo, Rajasthan (M.Ed.). retrieved https://www.gujaratuniversity.ac.in/publicationdata?deptid=11

Bhanegaonkar, M., & Mahfoodh, M. (2013). New approach for evaluating EFLM: An eclectic developed checklist. *International Journal of Scientific and Research Publications,* 3(10), 1-8.

Borg, W.R., & Gall, M.D. (1989). *Educational research: An introduction.* New York: Longman.

Brown, J.D. (1995). *The elements of language curriculum: A systematic approach to program development.* Boston: Heinle & Heinle.

Chaudhury, T.A., & Karim, M.Z. (2014). CLT approach in developing English reading skills in tertiary levels in Bangladesh. *Asian Journal of Education and e-Learning,* 2(1), 47-55.

Clement, P. (2008). Critical analysis of school science textbooks. *Science Education International,* 19, 93–96.

Delen, I., & Kesercioğlu, T. (2012). How middle school students' Science process skills affected by Turkey's national curriculum change? *Journal of Turkish Science Education.* 9. 3-9.

Deshmukh, N.D., & Deshmukh, V.M. (2011). *Textbook: A source of students' misconceptions at the secondary school level.* Retrieved from http://episteme4.hbcse.tifr.res.in/proceedings/strand-ii-cognitive-and-affective-studies-ofstme/deshmukh-deshmukh

Dipika, B.S. (2004). *Shaikshanik Sansodhan.* University Grantha Nirman Board, Ahmadabad, Gujarat.

Dudley-Evans., T., & St John, M., J. (1998). *Developments in English for specific purposes: A multi-disciplinary approach.* Cambridge: Cambridge University Press.

Duit, R., & Treagust, D.F. (2003). Learning in Science-from behaviourism towards social constructivism and beyond. In B.J. Fraser, & K.G. Tobin (Eds.), *International Handbook of Science Education.* Dordrecht: Kluwer academic press.

Edwards J. M. (2007). Evaluering van natuurwetenskaphandboekevir die onderrig van warmte in graad 7. MEd-verhandeling. Potchefstroom: Noord-Wes Universiteit.

Ensor, P., Dunne, T., Galant, J., Gumedze, F., Jaffer, S., Reeves, C., & Tawodzera, G. (2002). Textbooks, teaching and learning in primary mathematics classrooms. *African Journal of Research in SMT education,* 6, 21-35.

Erickson, G., & Tiberghien, A. (1989). Heat and temperature. In R. Driver, E. Guesne, G. L. Erickson, & A. Tiberghien (Eds.), *Children's ideas in science.* Philadelphia: Milton Keynes.

Erten, S., Şen, C. & Yüzüak, A.V.(2015). A critical analysis to 5th grade elementary Science education textbook. *International Journal of Humanities Social Sciences and Education,* 2(1), 60-65. Retrieved from www.arcjournals.org

Eugene, L. C., & David, A. F. (2007). Analysis of five high school Biology textbooks used in the United States for inclusion of the Nature of Science, *International Journal of Science Education*, 29(15), 1847-1868, DOI: 10.1080/09500690601159407

Fatima, G., Shah, S.K., & Sultan, H. (2015). Textbook analysis and evaluation of 7th & 8th grade in Pakistani context, *International Journal of English Language Teaching*, 3(4), 79-97.

Gilavand, A., Moosavi, A., Gilavand, M., & Moosavi, Z. (2016). Content analysis of the Science textbooks of Iranian junior high school course in terms of the components of health education. *International Journal of Paediatrics*, 4(12), 4057-69. DOI: 10.22038/ijp.2016.7428.Retrieved from https://pdfs.semanticscholar.org/32e7/b5d2401774dfc97a6fe3e6e32ecb4c39393e.pdf

Guilani, M.A., Yasin, M.S., & Hua, T.K. (2011). Authenticity of Iranian English textbooks for schools. *English Language and Literature Studies*, 1 (2), 25-30.

Helen, M. (2014). Socio-scientific issues and multidisciplinary in school Science textbooks, *International Journal of Science Education*, 36(7), 1137-1158, DOI :10.1080/09500693.2013.848493

Henson, K.T. (2004). *Constructive methods for teaching in diverse middle-level classrooms*, Allyn & Bacon, Boston, Massachusetts.

Hossain, M.E. (2010). *English for today, for classes 9-10: An empirical study.* BRAChttp://dx.doi.org/10.1063/1.1583534

Hubisz, J. (2003). Middle-school texts don't make the grade. *Physics Today*, 50-54.

Hutchinson, T. & Torres, E. (1994). The textbook as agent of change. *ELT Journal*, 48 (4), 315- 328.

Iszak, A., & Sherin, M.G. (2003). Exploring the use of new representations as a resource for teacher learning. *School Science and Mathematics 103*(1), 18–27.

Jahangard, A. (2007). The evaluation of the EFL materials taught at Iranian high schools. *The Asian EFL Journal*, 9 (2), 130- 150.

Jangaiah, C. (2007). Gender issues as focused in NCF 2005 with reference to secondary school textbooks of Andhra Pradesh. RIE (NCERT) Mysore.

Jayendra, P. J. (1990). A critical study of physics textbook of standard-11 of Gujarat state", Gujarat University, Ahmadabad (M.Ed.) retrieved from https://www.gujaratuniversity.ac.in/publicationdata?deptid=11

Jayshree, R.P. (1997). *An evaluation of Mathematics Textbooks for standard V, VI and VII published by Gujarat Board of School Textbooks.* Maharaja Sayajeerao University, Baroda.

K.G. Desai and H.G. Desai (1973), Sanshodhan nee Paddhatioane Pravidhio, University Grantha Nirman Board, Ahmadabad, Gujarat. retrieved from https://www.gujaratuniversity.ac.in/publicationdata?deptid=11

Kanaiyalal, P.D. (2007). Opinion of students and teachers towards Hindi textbook at secondary level, Gujarat University, Ahmadabad (M.Ed.). retrieved from https://www.gujaratuniversity.ac.in/publicationdata?deptid=11

Kaul, L. (2011). *Methodology of educational research.* New Delhi: Vikas Publishing House Pvt Ltd.

Kesidou, S., Roseman, J. E. (2002). How well do middle school Science programmes measure up? Findings from Project 2061's curriculum review. *Journal of Research in Science Teaching*, 39(6), 522–549.

Klassen, S. (2006). A theoretical framework for contextual Science teaching. Inter change 37(1-2), 31–62.

Knight, R.D. (2004). Physics for scientists and engineers. A strategic approach. San Francisco: Pearson Addison Wesley.

Koppal, M., & Caldwell, A. (2004). Meeting the challenge of science literacy: Project 2061 efforts to improve science education. Cell Biology Education, 3, 28–30.

Koppal, M., & Caldwell, A. (2004). Meeting the challenge of science literacy: Project 2061 efforts to improve science education. Cell Biology Education, 3, 28–30.

Krippendorff, K. (1980). *Content analysis: An introduction to its methodology.* Beverly Hills, CA: Sage

Kulm, G., Roseman, J., & Treistman, M. (1999). A benchmarks-based approach to textbook evaluation. Science books and films, Retrieved from http://www.project2061.org/publications/textbook/articles/approach.htm

Laabidi, H., & N Fissi, A. (2016). Fundamental criteria for effective textbook evaluation. *Asian-EFL Journal*, 1(2).

Lawrence, W.P.W. (2011). *Textbook evaluation: A framework for evaluating the fitness of the* Hong Kong New Secondary School Curriculum 2011.

Lawson, A.E. (1999). What should students learn about the nature of science and how should we teach it? Applying the "If-and-then-therefore" pattern to develop students' theoretical reasoning abilities in science. *Journal of College Science Teaching*, 28, 401-411.

Laxmisankar, S.P. (1997). A critical study of mathematics textbook of standard-12 of Gujarat state, Gujarat University, Ahmadabad (M.Ed.). retrieved fromhttps://www.gujaratuniversity.ac.in/publicationdata?deptid=11

Leedy, P.D., & Ormrod, J.E. (2005). *Practical research: Planning and design (8th ed.).* Upper Saddle River: Pearson Education.

Leite, L. (1999). Heat and temperature: an analysis of how these concepts are dealt with in textbooks. *European Journal of Teacher Education*, 22, 75-88. http://dx.doi.org/10.1080/0261976990220106

Lemmer, M., Edwards, J.A., & Rapule, S. (2008). Educators' selection and evaluation of Natural Science textbooks. *South African Journal of Education 28, 175–187.*

Lemmer, M., & Edwards, J.M. (2007). Evaluation of natural sciences textbooks. Paper presented at the SAIP conference, WITS University, Johannesburg, 2-5.

Leslie, E. S. (1988). Evaluating ELT textbooks and materials. *ELT Journal*, 42(4), 237–246.

Littlejohn, A. (1998). The analysis of language teaching materials: Inside the Trojan horse. In B. Tomlinson (Ed.) *Materials development in language teaching* (pp.190-216). Cambridge: Cambridge University Press.

Litz, D.R.A. (2000). Textbook evaluation and ELT management: A South Korean case study. *Asian EFL Journal, 1-53*. Retrieved in 2022 from http://www.asian-efl-journal.com/Litz_thesis.pdf.

Litz, D.R.A. (2001). Textbook evaluation and ELT management: *A South Korean case study. R*etrieved July, 2022 from http://www.pdfgeni.com,

Liu, Y., & Treagust, D. (2013). Content analysis of diagrams in secondary school Science textbooks. 10.1007/978-94-007-4168-3_14

Maheshwari, V.K. (2014). *Text books- An integral part of any educational system.* Retrieved July, 2022 from http://www.vkmaheshwari.com/WP/?p=2414

Mahfoodh, M.I.H.A., & Bhanegaonkar, S.G. (2013). New approach for evaluating EFLM (An eclectic developed checklist). *International Journal of Scientific and Research Publications, 3(10), 1-8.*

Mangal, S.K., & Mangal, S. (2013). *Research Methodology in Behavioural Sciences*. Delhi: PHI Learning Private Limited.

Mc Grath, I. (2002). *Materials evaluation and design for language teaching*. Edinburgh: Edinburgh University Press

Mc Grath, I. (2006). Teachers' and learners' images for course books. *ELT Journal,* 60(2), 171-180.

McKinney, D., & Michalovic, M. (2004). Teaching the stories of scientists and their discoveries. *The Science Teacher*, 46-51.

Mehulkumar, A.P. (2017). Opinions of students and teachers towards new Science and Technology textbook of standard 9 RET, International Academic Publishing, New Delhi

Miekley, J. (2005). ESL Textbook Evaluation Checklist. The Reading Matrix 5/2, 9-17.

Mishra. L. (2016) Focus Group Discussion in Qualitative Research *Techno Learn* Vol. 6: No. 1: p. 1-5 DOI: 10.5958/2249-5223.2016.00001.2

Mishra, M. (2016). A study of Science-Technology-Environment-Society components of Science and Technology curriculum and its effect on the development of higher order cognitive skills among the secondary students. (Doctoral dissertation). Retrieved from https://shodhganga.inflibnet.ac.in/handle/10603/198072

Moghtadi, L. (2014). Iranian high school EFL textbooks: Why they should be modified. *International Journal of Language Learning and Applied Linguistics World*, 5 (2), 53-69.

Mohd Arif, H.B., & Bilal, A.S. (2021). Evaluation of science textbook of Class VIII of Jammu and Kashmir state board of school education on the basis of responses of experts. *PJAEE,* 18(8)

Mousavi, Y., & Sabzalipou, B. (2013). The evaluation of Iranian high school English textbook from the prospective of students. *Journal of Basic and Applied Scientific Research,* 3(8), 481-484.

Mukundan, J., Hajimohammadi, R., & Nimehchisalem, V. (2011). Developing an English language textbook evaluation checklist. *Contemporary Issues in Education Research*, 4(6), 21. doi: 10.19030/cier. V 4i6.4383

National Curriculum Framework. (2005). *Position paper national focus group on teaching of Science*. New Delhi, India: National Council of Educational Research and Training (NCERT)

National Science Teachers Association. (2005). *The use and adoption of textbooks in science teaching*. Retrieved August 13, 2021, from http://www.nsta.org/textbooks

Nazeer, M., Shah, S.K., & Sarwat, Z. (2015). Evaluation of Oxon English textbook used in Pakistan public schools for 6th & 7th grade. *Journal for the Study of English Linguistics*, 3(1), 51-79.

NCERT (2000). Fifth Survey of Educational Research, Volume II New Delhi, NCERT, New Delhi.

NCERT (2007) Sixth Survey of Research in Education, Volume II, NCERT, New Delhi.

NCERT (2023) National Curriculum Framework for School Education

Newton, D.P., & Newton, L.D. (2006). Could elementary Mathematics textbooks help give attention to reasons in the classroom? *Educational Studies in Mathematics*, 64, 69–84.

Nguyen, C.T. (2015). An evaluation of the textbook English 6: A case study from secondary schools in the Mekong delta provinces of Vietnam, Doctoral Thesis, University of Sheffield March.

Nicol, C.C., & Crespo, S.M. (2006). Learning to teach with mathematics textbooks: How pre service teachers interpret and use curriculum materials. *Educational Studies in Mathematics*, 62, 331-355.http://dx.doi.org/10.1007/s10649-006-5423-y

Novak, J.D. (2004). Reflections on a half-century of thinking in science education and research: Implications from a twelve-year longitudinal study of children's learning. *Canadian Journal of Science, Mathematics and Technology*, 4, 23-41. http://dx.doi.org/10.1080/14926150409556595

Nunan, D. (1987). *The teacher as curriculum developer*. Adelaide: National Curriculum Resource Centre.

Ogan-Bekiroglu, F. (2007) To what degree do the currently used Physics textbooks meet the expectations? *Journal of Science Teacher Education* 18, 599–628.

Ogan-Bekiroglu, F. (2007) To what degree do the currently used Physics textbooks meet the expectations?, *Journal of Science Teacher Education* 18, 599–612

Ohman, A. (2005). Qualitative methodology for rehabilitation research. *Journal of Rehabilitation Medicine*, 37(5), 273-280.

O'Neill, R. (1982). Why use textbooks. *ELT Journal*, 36(2), 104-111.

Oppenheim, A.N. (1992). *Opinionnaire design, interviewing attitude measurement*. London: Pinter.

Osama, M.K., & Ismail, A. (2016). Evaluation of the third class Science text book from the teacher's perspective at Madaba Municipality *International Education Studies*, 9(3)

Papajani, J. (2015). The evaluation of the EFL textbooks used in the high schools of Elbasan, Albania. *European Journal of Language and Literature*, 1(1), 7-15.

Parthasarathy,J.&Premalatha,T.LiZhao(Reviewingeditor)(2022)Contentanalysis ofvisualrepresentationsinbiologytextbooksacrossselectededucationalboards from Asia, Cogent Education, 9:1, DOI: 10.1080/2331186X.2022.2057002

Paresh, K.J.P. (1995). A critical study of Chemistry textbook of standard-11 of Gujarat state. Gujarat University, Ahmadabad (M.Ed.) dissertation Retrieved from https://www.researchgate.net/publication/262469583_An_analysis_of_grade_six_textbook_on_electricity_through_content_analysis_and_student_writing_responses

Patel,U.A.(2009).AcriticalstudyofChemistrytextbookofstandard-11ofGujaratstate. Jain Vishvabharati Vishvavidyalay, Ladnoo, Rajasthan (M.Ed.). dissertation Retrieved from https://www.researchgate.net/publication/262469583_An_analysis_of_grade_six_textbook_on_electricity_through_content_analysis_and_student_writing_responses

Patel, D.S. (2017). Significance of materials development in language teaching. *A Journal of Teaching English Language and Literature*. Retrieved from https://www.researchgate.net/publication/262469583_An_analysis_of_grade_six_textbook_on_electricity_through_content_analysis_and_student_writing_responses

Peter, N. (2000). Representations of indigenous knowledge in secondary school Science textbooks in Australia and Canada. *International Journal of Science Education*, 22(6), 603-617, DOI: 10.1080/095006900289697

Position Paper. (2005). National focus group on teaching of Science, NCERT, New Delhi.

Qadeer, A. (2013). An analysis of grade six textbook on electricity through content analysis and student writing responses. *Revista Brasileira de Ensino de Fısica*, 35(1), 1501. Retrieved from https://www.researchgate.net/publication/262469583_An_analysis_of_grade_six_textbook_on_electricity_through_content_analysis_and_student_writing_responses

Qasim, S.H., & Pandey, S.S. (2017). Content analysis of diagrammatic representations in upper primary Science textbooks. *International Journal of Research – Granthaalayah*, 5(7), 474-479. https://doi.org/10.5281/zenodo.838939.

Rahimi, M., & Hassani, M. (2012). Attitude towards EFL textbooks as a predictor of attitude towards learning English as a foreign language. *Procedia – Social and Behavioural Sciences*, 31, 66–72.

Rahimpour, M., & Hashemi, R. (2011). Textbook selection and evaluation in EFL context. *World Journal of Education*, 1 (2), 62-68.

Rashid, A. (2013). An evaluation study of science textbooks of Class VIII-X in the context of Environmental awareness (Doctoral dissertation). Retrieved from http://shodhganga.inflibnet.ac.in:8080/jspui/handle/10603/276915

Razmjoo, S.A. (2010). Developing a textbook evaluation scheme for the expanding circle. *Iranian Journal of Applied Language Studies*, 2(1), 121-136.

Razmjoo, S.A. (2007). High schools or private institutes' textbooks? Which fulfil communicative language teaching principles in the Iranian context? *The Asian EFL Journal Quarterly*, 9 (4), 125-139.

Richards, J.C. (2001). *Curriculum development in language teaching*. Cambridge: Cambridge University Press.

Roopa, R.T.S. (2008). Values in secondary school Science education: An analysis of curricular objectives and perceptions of teachers and students. (Doctoral dissertation). Retrieved from https://shodhganga.inflibnet.ac.in/handle/10603/17638

Sabzalipour, B., & Mousavi, Y. (2013). The evaluation of Iranian high school English textbook from the prospective of students. *Journal of Basic and Applied Scientific Research*, 3(8), 481-484.

Sarita, S. (2010). The assessment of the quality of science education textbooks: Conceptual framework and instruments for analysis Ph.D. thesis at University of South Africa

Sayre, E. (2013). Integrated Student-Cantered Learning to Promote Critical Thinking in High School Social Studies Classrooms (Graduate Thesis). Retrieved December 02, 2015, from http://etd.fcla.edu/CF/CFH0004486/Sayre_Elaine_N_201308_BS.pdf

Senem, B.Y. (2013). Content analysis of 9th grade Physics curriculum, textbook, lessons with respect to science process skills. (Doctoral dissertation). Retrieved from http://etd.lib.metu.edu.tr/upload/12616599/index.pdf

Shabani, M.B., & Mansoori, N.A. (2013). An evaluation of the third-grade high school English textbook: An Iranian case study. *Journal of Studies in Social Sciences*, 2 (1), 67-80.

Shafiee, N. S. (2012). An evaluation of a global ELT textbook in Iran: A two-phase approach. *International Journal of Humanities and Social Science*, 2 (3), 184-191.

Shahmohammadi, N. (2013). Content analysis of elementary Science textbooks based on the achievement motivation constructs. *Procedia — Social and Behavioural Sciences*, 84, 426 – 430. Retrieved from www.sciencedirect.com

Sharma, R. (2017). Content analysis of 6th grade NCERT Science textbook to study the scope of developing desirable values in students. *Scholarly Research Journal for Humanity Science and English Language.* Retrieved from https://www.srjis.com/pages/pdfFiles/15436545583.%20Dr.%20Rachna%20Sharma.pdf

Sharma, R. (2017). Content analysis of 6th grade NCERT Science Textbook to Study the Scope of Developing Desirable Values in Students. *Scholarly Research Journal for Humanity Science and English Language.* Retrieved from https://www.srjis.com/pages/pdfFiles/15436545583.%20Dr.%20Rachna%20Sharma.pdf

Sheldon, L.E. (1987). *ESL textbooks and materials: Problems in evaluation and development.* Oxford University Press: Modern English Publications.

Sheldon, L.E. (1988). Evaluating ELT textbooks and materials. *ELT Journal*, 42 (2), 237-246.

Singh, A.K. (2018). *Tests, measurements and research methods in Behavioral Sciences.* New Delhi: Bharti Bhawan.

Sinha, M.P., & Tripathy, H.H. (2005). A study of correlation of the curriculum load in science for classes IX and X. *Indian Educational Review*, 41.

Skierso, A. (1991). Textbook selection and evaluation. In M. Celce-Murcia (Ed.), *Teaching English as a second or foreign language* (pp. 432-453). Boston: Heinle & Heinle Publishers.

Sogo, A., & Spernjak, A. (2012). Practical Work in Biology, Chemistry and Physics at Lower Secondary and General Upper Secondary Schools in Slovenia. *Eurasia Journal of Mathematics, Science & Technology Education*, 8(1), 11-19. Retrieved November 29, 2015, from http://www.ejmste.com/v8n1/eurasia_v8n1_sorgo.pdf

Sundararaman, I. (2018). Gender matters in science learning: An analysis of experiences and aspirations in an urban context (Doctoral dissertation). Retrieved from http://shodhganga.inflibnet.ac.in:8080/jspui/handle/10603/257571

Tarannum, S. (2015). The authenticity gap between what is taught in Bangladeshi EFL Courses and the Reality of authentic English. *IIUC Studies*, 12, 101-110.

Tok, H. (2010). TEFL textbook evaluation: From teachers' perspectives. *Educational Research and Review*, 5(9), 508-517.

Tomlinson, B. (2011). *Introduction: Principles and procedures of materials development.* Cambridge: Cambridge University Press

Tomlinson, B. (1999). Developing criteria for evaluating L2 materials. *IATEFL Issues*, 147, 10-13.

Tomlinson, B. (2003). Materials evaluation. In B. Tomlinson (Ed.), *Developing materials for language teaching* (pp. 15-36). London: Continuum.

Tomlinson, B., Dat, B., Masuhara, H., & Rubdy, R. (2001). ELT courses for adults. *ELT Journal*, 55(1), 80-90 *University Journal, Special Issue* (01), 112–127.

Tron, B. (2016). An analysis of the Science syllabus prescribed for the secondary school level in the state of Meghalaya, *South-Asian Journal of*

Multidisciplinary Studies, 4(6), 245-246. Retrieved from http://sajms.com/wpcontent/uploads/2017/09/An_Analysis_of_the_Science_Syllabus_at_the_Secondary_school_Level.pdf

Umesh, D.R., & Tarisai, C. (2016). An analysis of South African Grade 9 Natural Sciences textbooks for their representation of nature of science. *International Journal of Science Education*, DOI: 10.1080/09500693.201

Ur, P. (1996). *A course in language teaching: Practice and theory.* Cambridge: Cambridge University Press.

Vanden,B.G.(2004).DieGeleenthedewatuitkomsgebaseerdetaalhandboekebiedvir die antikilling van leaders se meervoudigeintelligensies, Ph.D. thesis, University of South Africa.

Vijay, K.B. (2008). To evaluate the textbook of Guajarati subject for standard-9 of Gujarat state", Bhavnagar University Bhavnagar (M.Ed.). Retrieved from https://www.researchgate.net/publication/262469583_

Zacharias, N. (2005). Teachers' beliefs about internationally-published materials: A survey of tertiary English teachers in Indonesia. *RELC Journal*, 36(1), 23-36.

Zohrabi, M., Sabouri, H., & Kheradmand, M. (2014). Comparative study of Interchange1 and English book1 of Iranian high schools. *Education International Journal of English,* 3(2), 95-10